Dr. Young's
Guide *to*

DEMOTIVATING EMPLOYEES

How to Dispirit, Dishearten and
Demoralize Your Workers

Also by Mark Geoffrey Young

The West Australian Joke Book

*How to Promote Your Business: The Easy Guide to
Public Relations*

Dr. Young's
Guide *to*
DEMOTIVATING EMPLOYEES

How to Dispirit, Dishearten and
Demoralize Your Workers

By Mark Geoffrey Young
Illustrated by T. R. Patrick

Dolyttle & Seamore
New York, NY

Dr. Young's Guide to Demotivating Employees
By Mark Geoffrey Young
Illustrations by T. R. Patrick

Dolyttle & Seamore
New York

Dolyttle & Seamore
345 West 85th Street
Suite 43
New York, NY 10024

Visit our websites at www.demotivationist.com and www.dolyttle.com

Library of Congress Control Number: 2007904951

Publisher's Cataloging-in-Publication Data

Young, Mark Geoffrey.

Dr. Young's Guide to Demotivating Employees: How to Dispirit, Dishearten, and Demoralize Your Workers / by Mark Geoffrey Young; illustrated by T.R. Patrick.

p. cm.
ISBN-13: 978-0-9797782-3-0
ISBN-10: 0-9797782-3-0

1. Business — Humor.   2. Success – Humor.
3. Self-help techniques – Humor.   4. Management – Humor.

I. Patrick, T.R.   II. Title.

PN6231.B85Y68 2008
818'.54 dc22

Manufactured in the United States of America

10 9 8 7 6 5 4 3 2 1

To Mike and Mark,
who taught me everything there is to know about demotivation.

TABLE OF CONTENTS

PREFACE

I started writing this book while I was working for a small company that was filled with more unhappy employees than I'd ever encountered in one place. In fact, every person who worked for this organization talked about quitting on a daily basis. Few of them did.

While most organizations would be concerned about this state of affairs, the owners simply swept the problem under the carpet and did absolutely nothing. Why? They knew that there was no such thing as a talented, happy, worker (all talented employees are bosses) and used this to their advantage.

Rather than trying to motivate their workers with bonuses, raises and incentives, these innovative thinkers demotivated their workers with platitudes, insults and uncaring comments—and watched their income grow. Instead of dealing with worker complaints, they tackled the real issues—increasing profits, reducing costs and coming up with ways to make their employees work harder.

While their workers may have been unhappy, the owners knew that very few of them would ever leave. Why? They were scared. While the workers' jobs may have been meaningless, the employees earned enough to pay their mortgage, feed their families and make the minimum monthly payments on their credit cards—even if some of them had to work a second job.

What surprised me the most, was the fact that almost all the workers were resigned to their fate. While the employees would have liked the owners to speak with them, they didn't expect it. The owners used this to their advantage by getting nastier and meaner at every opportunity, hoping that their fat, lazy employees would pack their bags and walk out the door, so they could be replaced with cheaper models who would work harder.

If this sounds like a bad way to do business, ask yourself: are you in business to make friends or money? If the answer is to make money, keep reading. If not, put this book down and enroll in one of those expensive seminars that shows you how to motivate your employees so they can take advantage of you, your niceness and your company.

Dr. Mark Geoffrey Young

New York, New York

When I got a call from Mark Young asking me if I would like to write the forward to his book, I was quite surprised. Mostly surprised because I had no idea who he was! But then he told me that we once shared the last pretzel at a press gathering some eleven years earlier. Oh, that Mark Young! He explained he was writing a book and needed someone famous to write the forward.

He further explained that so far he wasn't able to find anyone famous who would do it, and he was now down to the contacts on his "D" list. But he assured me there was an "E" and an "F" list too, so I wasn't his last hope.

When I asked what writing the forward involved, Mark was clear and concise. "You do it for free," he said. "I'm up against a deadline, so you have to do it for free and you have to do it fast. I basically need to mention in **bold type** that you're **MAD Magazine's Maddest Writer** and **The Giz Wiz** on **radio** and **TV**. And that you have a daily Podcast that gets hundreds of thousands of downloads a month. They're not the most impressive credentials, but you're all I got for now."

Okay, so I'm thinking to myself, "This guy is honest, but he sure doesn't make it sound very interesting. I mean why would I bother?" Before hanging up I figured I'd ask what the book was about. "Oh my book is all about demotivation," Mark said excitedly. "All about making people not want to do stuff." Hmmm. He sure made me not want to write the intro to his book so I guess he knows his subject pretty well!

Bottom line? If Mark doesn't sucker someone else on the E & F list into writing a better forward, this is most likely what you'll find at the front of his book!

Dick DeBartolo

MAD Magazine's Maddest Writer and The Giz Wiz.

www.gizwizbiz.com

THE WORLD'S 25 GREATEST DEMOTIVATORS

"Realizing that your workers are ignorant and unable to achieve anything without your help, makes it easier for you to obtain a feeling of superiority."
—Dr. Mark Geoffrey Young

Randy Newman
Josef Stalin
Dana Plato
Augusto Pinochet
Mao Tse-Tung
Donald Trump
Pol Pot
Leona Helmsley
Idi Amin Dada
Naomi Campbell
Benito Mussolini
Britney Spears
Saddam Hussein

Imelda Marcos
Osama Bin Laden
Genghis Khan
Francisco Franco
Nicolae Ceausesco
Gary Coleman
Paris Hilton
Manuel Noriega
Charles Manson
Anna Nicole Smith
Lindsey Lohan
David Berkowitz

DEFINITIONS

De·mot·i·vate *v.* The ability to inspire people to ignore a specific subject or topic and take absolutely no action in this area.

De·mot·i·vat·ed *adj.* Affected or marked by being unable to take action in a specific area or areas.

De·mot·i·vat·ion *n.* The act of inspiring people to take absolutely no action on a specific topic or topics, regardless of how hopeful the situation may appear.

De·mot·i·va·tion·ism *n.* The art and science of demotivation.

De·mot·i·va·tion·al·ism *(British variant of* **Demotivationism.** *This term is used by all members of the Commonwealth of Nations with the exception of Australia, Canada and Grenada).*

De·mot·i·va·tion·ist *n.* A person who inspires people to accept their menial position in society and helps them realize that they should make the most of what they have, as their situation is unlikely to change.

De·mot·i·va·tion·al·ist *(British variant of* **Demotivationist.** *This term is used by all members of the Commonwealth of Nations with the exception of Australia, Canada and Grenada).*

De·mot·i·va·tion·ists *n.* An obscure nineteenth-century cult organized by large American landowners that was devoted to discouraging enthusiasm, entrepreneurialism and vision amongst slaves, indentured workers and small-scale farmers.

INTRODUCTION

WHY SHOULD YOU DEMOTIVATE YOUR WORKERS?

"I've worked for assholes all my life. Now it's my turn to be the asshole."
–Dr. Mark Geoffrey Young

Nobody can deny that the workforce has undergone dramatic changes over the last thirty years. And all of these changes have cost you, the employer, money. Even though your employees are totally coddled and have it easier than ever before, they're still not happy. Just look at the benefits your workers get: sick days, paid vacation days, personal time and maternity leave, to mention a few. And no matter how much you give, your employees keep taking.

This book is designed to help restore you to your rightful position in the workplace—that of a god. People respect gods. They don't argue with gods. They don't complain that they're not fair. In fact, they expect gods to be unfair.

The sooner you put yourself on this pedestal, the happier you'll be—and the less you'll have to deal with your workers. Instead of coming to you with problems and badgering you with questions, your staff will keep their distance and give you the respect you think you've earned.

This will work wonders for your business. Rather than wasting time motivating your workers and showing them how "valuable" they are, you'll be able to concentrate on the real issues: squeezing productivity gains out of them and getting them to make more money for you. While this book is designed to help you deal with employees, feel free to use these techniques to manage your families, friends and clients.

Your employees think that they are your most valuable asset. This is a myth perpetrated by the media. If you allow your workers to believe this, they'll take advantage of you and your niceness at every opportunity. By striking back and showing your people how worthless they truly are—and how easy they are to replace—you'll be able to wring more out of each and every employee. The fear of being tossed out with the garbage will inspire them to work harder. If you're worried that they won't like you, stop worrying. The only reason they turn up now is because you pay them.

As soon as employees realize that you, and only you, are responsible for your company's success, they'll stop whining and get to work! Not only will productivity soar, you'll look more successful. And yes, you're the one who will be able to claim credit for these miracles. Remember, if you're successful, your workers are successful. And they'll live fuller, happier lives knowing that even though they've got tiny insignificant jobs, they're contributing in a small way to a glorious enterprise led by a business genius.

Implementing this wisdom takes forethought and practice. While the skills you will acquire from this book are a step in the right direction, they're only the beginning. If you really want to get results, consider hiring a Demotivationist™ to analyze your company and advise you on the best way to get back in the drivers seat. While this may be expensive, it's a lot cheaper than wasting your money motivating your workers.

Hiring and Training Workers

"Always focus on what you want your workers to achieve and work out the easiest way to get them do it."—Dr. Mark Geoffrey Young

Hiring great workers is the best way to increase your profits. But, the sad fact is that there's no such thing as great employees. Anybody who could be a great worker is a boss. Since there's no way to hire good employees, do the next best thing: hire cheap workers.

But remember, just because you're buying cheap doesn't mean you have to settle. Because workers need you more than you need them, they'll go to great lengths to prove themselves. Use this knowledge by getting every potential employee to prove their worth before you place them on your payroll. Instead of hiring the person who appears to be the best, get each applicant to volunteer at your company before you make a decision. Give them several real assignments and show their work to your clients. If your customers don't realize that it's not your work, offer the lucky candidate a job.

If several applicants pass this test, hold a reverse auction and get them to bid against each other for the job. Hiring the lowest bidder not only saves you money, it shows workers their true value—and how easy they are to replace.

———•———

When filling an open position, never ask your existing workers about the qualifications or skills needed for that job. This is especially true if you have no expertise in that area.

———•———

Let potential workers know that the company operates on "boss time" by showing up thirty minutes after the scheduled time for the interview. Don't apologize for being late, as it sets a bad precedent for the future.

———•———

When interviewing a potential worker, assert your position of superiority by refusing to shake their hand. You'll also reduce the risk of getting sick if you enforce this policy throughout the company with your existing employees.

———•———

Give potential workers brochures and other information about your company when you interview them for the first time. Test them on their company knowledge during the second interview.

———•———

Reduce conflicts and prevent future arguments by never hiring anyone who appears to be more intelligent than you. Face facts, if they were smarter than you, they'd be working for themselves.

———•———

Reduce the chance of an applicant turning down a job with your organization by refusing to allow them to meet any of your existing employees. Allowing your workers to meet a candidate before you make a decision gives them the impression that you value their opinions.

———•———

Cut your training costs by getting all candidates to complete a one-week, on-site "training course" before you decide who to hire. Charge all applicants a fee for the upheaval they cause and reject anybody who is unwilling to submit to this test.

———•———

Don't tell the section leader when a new worker is starting, as this will encourage him or her to relax and stockpile work for your new employee.

———•———

Reduce the demands a new hire places on your time by wearing old, dirty clothing on the day he or she starts. If you smell bad, they'll quickly find another "go to" person when they have a problem.

———•———

Don't waste time training new workers on the "ins" and "outs" of their new position. If the successful candidate has all of the skills they claim, they should be able to do everything the minute they start.

———•———

Have new workers arrive at least thirty minutes early on their first day. Getting them to spend time in the lobby watching their coworkers arrive for work makes it easier for them to integrate.

———•———

Encourage your new workers to become independent the moment they start work by refusing to show them where the bathrooms, conference rooms and supplies are located. Industrious workers will quickly locate everything they need on their own.

———•———

Never introduce new workers to your existing staff as it encourages them to waste time gossiping instead of working. Keeping things on a professional level encourages your new employees to spend the time needed to learn their job.

———•———

Do payroll and other HR procedures when you have time. If the worker is unhappy with the standard four to six week wait for their first paycheck, they're not going to fit into your company.

———•———

Issue new workers with your standard fifteen-page employment contract after their first week of work. Don't worry if it seems overly complex—employees expect these agreements be set in six-point type and written in legalese.

———•———

Help new workers handle their jobs better and acquire new skills by scheduling voluntary training sessions at the end of each workday. Let them know how critical each of these sessions is to their development and continued employment.

———•———

Prepare for your move offshore by requiring every employee to learn Hindi. This makes it easier for your workers to train their replacements.

ACTION! ITEMS

- ✘ *DO* NOT! ask your existing workers about the skills needed for an open position.

- ✘ *TURN!* up thirty minutes late to hiring interviews.

- ✘ *NEVER!* shake hands with a potential employee.

- ✘ *TEST!* applicants about their knowledge of your company.

- ✘ *REFUSE!* to hire anybody who appears smarter than you.

- ✘ *NEVER!* allow applicants to meet your existing employees.

- ✘ *DEMAND!* all applicants complete one week of unpaid training.

- ✘ *ALWAYS!* refuse to tell the section leader when their new worker is starting.

- ✘ *WEAR!* dirty clothing to reduce interaction with workers.

- ✘ *AVOID!* training new hires as they should be able to do everything without help or guidance.

- ✘ *GET!* new hires to spend their first thirty minutes in the lobby.

- ✘ *ALLOW!* new employees to find supplies, bathrooms and facilities on their own.

- ✘ *PREVENT!* existing employees from introducing themselves to your new worker.

- ✘ *DO!* payroll when you have time. A six-week wait for the first check is reasonable.

- ✘ *ISSUE!* new workers with your standard fifteen-page employment agreement after their first week.

- ✘ *SCHEDULE!* voluntary training sessions at the end of each day.

- ✘ *MAKE!* it easier to move offshore by requiring all workers to understand Hindi.

COMMUNICATING WITH YOUR WORKERS

"The worst mistake a boss can make is to say 'well done.'"
—Dr. Mark Geoffrey Young

Now that you've hired and trained your new workers, you have to work out how you're going to communicate with them. The best way is to stay as far away from your employees as humanly possible. Encouraging underlings to speak with you is almost as bad as swimming in a pond with a hungry alligator because they both want a piece of you.

As well as avoiding contact with your workers, remember that your employees are not your friends. If you believe that they like you because they laugh at your jokes and speak to you civilly, you won't be the boss for long. Remember, the only reason they show up for work is because you pay them. Put simply, they don't like you any more than you like them.

Repay this hostility with hostility. Put your feelings aside and avoid their problems like the plague. Speak to them only when necessary. Keep your office door closed. Walk as quickly as possible through the office. Avoid eye contact. The key to your success is ignoring your workers at every opportunity. When you do have to communicate with them, do it by email or telepathy.

—•—

Make your employees more productive by sharing as little information with them as possible. As well as keeping them focused on their jobs, they'll interact with you a lot less if they're forced to develop their own research skills.

—•—

Allow all of your calls to go into voicemail and return them in a single session at a different time each day. By being constantly unavailable, you'll encourage your employees and clients to deal with their own problems, instead of running to you for the answer.

—•—

Encourage communication between employees by getting everybody to wear a tag with their name and title on it. This not only makes it seem like you know everybody's name, you can instantly see the office hierarchy—and decide if you should even acknowledge a particular worker's presence.

—•—

Prevent people stabbing each other in the back by removing all of your company's suggestion boxes. Allowing workers to make unsolicited comments only encourages them to put forward costly, impractical ideas.

—•—

Install suggestion boxes wherever possible. This not only encourages your employees to put forward anonymous ideas, it allows you to take credit for every unsolicited suggestion that's implemented.

———•———

Maintain the balance between management and staff by never smiling or saying hello to workers when you pass them in the hallway or parking lot. While this may appear rude, it's a lot better than having to deal with their problems and inane ideas.

———•———

No matter how large your company is, or how many people you employ, never waste time sending out news through employee newsletters and email blasts. Workers who really need information will always find what they're looking for.

———•———

Reduce the chance of germs spreading through the office by always using the intercom when you need to communicate with a worker—regardless of how close you are to their desk.

———•———

Improve your productivity by insisting that your workers make themselves available 24/7. Do this by requiring everybody to purchase their own cell phone.

———•———

Workers are often afraid to ask for your input. Prevent this from happening by eavesdropping on their telephone calls and water-cooler conversations. Put forward your ideas before they feel compelled to ask for your opinion.

———•———

Remind your employees that you're the boss by making decisions before you get their input. You can always change your mind later if the facts don't match your opinions.

ACTION! ITEMS

✗ *PROVIDE!* your workers with as little information as possible.

✗ *ALLOW!* your telephone calls to go to voicemail and respond once per day.

✗ *GET!* everybody to wear a tag with their name and title on it.

✗ *REMOVE!* all suggestion boxes to prevent workers making inappropriate suggestions.

✗ *INSTALL!* suggestion boxes so workers can put forward ideas that can be used without attribution.

✗ *NEVER!* smile or say hello to workers when you pass them in the hallway or parking lot.

✗ *ELIMINATE!* newsletters and mass emails.

✗ *USE!* the intercom to prevent the spread of germs.

✗ *INSIST!* that workers who are on call purchase their own cell phones.

✗ *EAVESDROP!* on phone calls and conversations.

✗ *DON'T!* wait for all the facts before making a decision.

Asserting Your Leadership

"Leadership is the art of getting others to do the work you don't want to do."
—Dr. Mark Geoffrey Young

Congratulations, you now have all of the communication skills needed to succeed. The next step is to assert yourself as the leader and show your workers that you're in command. This means taking charge and accepting responsibility for every decision that turns out to be right. That's right, EVERY DECISION.

Weak leaders will see this as egotistical, but remember, that's why you're so much better than they are. Don't let your lack of expertise, skills or education prevent you from taking credit for everything good that occurs within your organization. Despite what you were told about sharing when you were growing up, sharing credit always costs you money in the form of raises and bonuses.

Sharing is equally bad when it comes to blame. Remember, you're the boss and you don't make mistakes. Get this point across to your workers by quickly pointing your finger at the person who you believe made the error. Getting your workers to admit their mistakes in front of everybody greatly reduces the number of errors they'll make in the future—and places you yet another rung above your employees.

———

Revitalize your long-term employees by making changes to their job quickly—and without consultation—before they have a chance to resist. Allowing them to comment and make decisions about their careers undermines your authority.

———

Show how good a leader you are by regularly taking an interest in your younger workers and their career paths. Every time you pass an employee in the hallway, ask him or her the same questions about their background, skills and experience.

———

Let your workers know that it's their job to make you look good—because if you look bad, everybody looks bad. Remind them that if this happens, they'll be out on the street looking for another job.

———

Let your workers see how you relate to the common people by telling jokes and stories about the people who work for you.

———

Show your employees how smart you are by using jargon, big words and technical terms whenever possible. Don't worry if you don't know their meaning or pronunciation—neither will your workers.

———

Help your employees get through the rough patches by discussing their confidential problems and challenges with them in the hallway or kitchen.

———•———

Keep a close eye on every task that your employees are working on and offer your input when you think it's needed. When the job is completed, get them to point out your contribution to other employees.

———•———

A good boss goes above and beyond what's required. Show your workers how much you appreciate their services by inviting them to stop by your office for advice on how they can do their jobs better after they finish work.

———•———

Give your long-serving workers autonomy by allowing them to make small, insignificant decisions that have absolutely no effect on your business. This helps them to feel like they're part of the team and makes their mundane jobs more interesting.

———•———

While only you can make decisions, get your lower-level employees involved in the process. Even though this may appear to be a waste of time, it offers you convenient scapegoats if something goes wrong.

———•———

Workers have no idea how hard you work or the great challenges you face as the boss. Let them know by mentioning how easy your job would be if you had competent employees.

———•———

Let workers know that you're watching them by installing surveillance cameras above every desk and connecting them to the Internet. Call employees at random and ask why they're not at their desk, or how come they're checking their personal email.

———•———

When you want to shock an employee into action, tell him or her that their performance is sub-par and if things don't improve you're going to let them go in 45 days. To improve moral, never mention the conversation again.

———•———

Show how progressive you are by instituting a casual dress code for your workers. Let them know that they're being watched by commenting frequently about what they're wearing.

———•———

Use your management skills to the fullest by sending out negative emails on Friday afternoons after your workers have gone home for the weekend. When they arrive at work on Monday, it will set the tone for the week. This is especially effective on holiday weekends.

———•———

When you ask a worker to update you on an issue—and they try to give you the facts—scream that you want the headline, not the feature story.

———•———

ACTION! ITEMS

- ✗ *MAKE!* changes to your workers' jobs without their input.

- ✗ *TAKE!* an interest in your workers by questioning them frequently about their skills.

- ✗ *REMIND!* employees that it's their job to make you look good.

- ✗ *TELL!* jokes and stories about your workers.

- ✗ *SHOW!* workers how smart you are by using jargon and technical terms.

- ✗ *DISCUSS!* confidential problems in the kitchen or hallway.

- ✗ *HAVE!* workers acknowledge your input frequently.

- ✗ *ADVISE!* your workers how to do their jobs better.

- ✗ *ALLOW!* workers to make menial decisions that don't impact your business.

- ✗ *GET!* employees involved in every decision to share the blame.

- ✗ *LET!* your workers know how easy your job would be if you had competent employees.

- ✗ *ENCOURAGE!* your workers to spend more time working by installing cameras over every desk.

- ✗ *TELL!* an employee that their performance is unsatisfactory and never mention the conversation again.

- ✗ *COMMENT!* frequently about what your workers are wearing.

- ✗ *SEND!* out negative emails on Friday afternoons to set the next week's tone.

- ✗ *SCREAM!* you only want the headline when an employee tries to give you all the facts.

Motivating Your Workers

Now that you know how to assert your authority, the next step is getting your employees to work harder. This means motivating your workers. If this sounds like a contradiction, it is, but in order to demotivate your workers, you must first motivate them.

There are two ways to do this. The traditional method is to offer those employees who do their job a bonus for simply turning up and doing what you're already paying them to do—in other words—paying them twice. While this is effective, it's costly and inefficient.

The second method is to motivate your staff by using fear as a weapon. Instead of offering trips to exotic locations, allow employees who meet your expectations to keep their jobs—if they promise to work harder. Do this by adjusting their quotas upwards each month until they hit breaking point and leave. When this happens, replace them with cheaper workers.

Over time workers often realize that their job is meaningless and lose enthusiasm. Prevent this from happening by reminding them continually that no matter how well they perform, or how hard they work, that you'll never be satisfied with their output.

Never compliment a worker because the minute you do is the moment they take their job for granted. Instead of offering praise, turn the situation around and find a fault—no matter how small—with at least one aspect of what they've done.

When a worker must be praised, do it in private without any witnesses. This will prevent your words being used against you in future salary negotiations.

If there's no way to avoid praising a worker in public, do it through a third-party. If you do something once it becomes company policy and you're forced to do it continually.

Challenge employees with boring, meaningless jobs by deliberately placing obstacles in their way. Not only will they work harder to meet your expectations, they'll obtain a sense of accomplishment when they finally get to where they're going.

Maintain the company spirit by getting your workers to sign an agreement recognizing the fact that anything they invent, write or develop during their employment—even if it occurs outside of work—belongs to your company.

———•———

Whenever your revenues exceed expectations, and your workers feel they're entitled to share in the rewards, kill the conversation by reminding them that even though interns could do their jobs, you have no intention of laying anybody off.

———•———

If revenues fall, inform your employees that it's because they're not working hard enough. Let them know that if their attitudes don't improve, you'll be forced to lay off workers.

———•———

Get your employees to go the extra mile by hiring a private investigator to uncover information about them. Threaten to reveal this to their family and friends if they fail to meet your new, higher, expectations.

———•———

Motivate your workers by letting them know that not only are you a great business leader, you're also great in bed. Pass on any tips you have to help them improve their home life—so they can be more productive at work.

———•———

Titles are great motivators. Keep your employees working hard by allocating—and reallocating—titles, based on their contribution to your company that month.

———•———

Let workers know that you're monitoring their progress by holding quarterly reviews with them and their supervisor. Use this opportunity to find fault with both the way they do their job—and with the way their supervisor manages them.

———•———

Motivate your employees to keep working through the winter by announcing bonuses in December and paying them in June—just before your workers take their annual vacations.

———•———

Small incentives are a great way to motivate your workers. Allow employees who do their job well to choose their own pens from the samples you've received.

———•———

Reward your workers by giving them discounts to the local dental, medical, hair and beauty schools. As well as your staff looking and feeling great, you'll feel good knowing that you're helping to train the next generation of leaders.

———•———

Let employees know how important their jobs are by telling them how you built the business without anybody's help or support. This is an especially effective motivator after they've just finished a rush job or worked through the weekend to meet a deadline.

———•———

Use fear to get your employees to work harder. Instead of issuing verbal threats, simply scatter a few pamphlets that mention the advantages of overseas outsourcing throughout your office.

———•———

Motivate your workers to sell more by telling them that unless they sell $10,000 worth of goods in the next four hours, you're going to close down the company. Do this often for maximum effect.

———•———

Whenever you feel a worker is going to ask for a raise, inspire him or her to work harder by praising a former employee. Talk about their predecessor's work ethic, loyalty and his or her ability to make the impossible happen.

———•———

Prevent your workers from resting on their laurels when they break a production record. Instead of praising them for doing a great job, complain loudly that if they were able to once, they should be able to do it every time.

———•———

Encourage your employees to work harder by placing a grade on every piece of work your employees hand in. This will inspire them to try harder as everybody wants an "A."

———•———

Keep your employees' egos in check by constantly asking them questions about their outside interests. If a worker wins an award, ask him or her if they had a relative on the panel, or if they dated one of the judges.

———•———

Get your employees to work harder by insisting that they teach their job to one of your summer interns. If the worker misbehaves in the future, threaten to bring the intern back.

———•———

Motivate your workers to constantly improve their writing skills by continually editing their work. Make revisions to every version—even if the document is acceptable.

———•———

Reward those workers who complete their tasks early and have time to stand around talking by giving them more work to complete.

———•———

If you employ workers with foreign accents, complain loudly that you can't understand a word that they're saying. Tell them if they don't learn English, you're going to replace them. This is especially effective with Canadians, Australians and British citizens.

————•————

When an employee gets a difficult issue under control, show your appreciation by reallocating this task to another employee and moving them to an area that makes better use of their skills.

————•————

If a worker makes a decision, question him or her thoroughly about why they've chosen that course of action. Use the opportunity to remind them about all of their other incorrect decisions.

————•————

Feel free to smoke or eat whenever you work closely with an employee. Remember, you're exempt from the normal rules of etiquette, and that the government's smoking regulations don't apply because you're the boss.

————•————

ACTION! ITEMS

- ✗ *TELL!* your workers that you'll never be happy with the work they produce.

- ✗ *NEVER!* praise a worker, instead turn the conversation around and find a fault.

- ✗ *IF!* you must praise an employee, do it in private.

- ✗ *SHOULD!* a worker need to be praised, always do it through a third-party.

- ✗ *CHALLENGE!* your workers by placing obstacles in their way.

- ✗ *GET!* workers to sign contracts saying the company owns everything they produce.

- ✗ *REMIND!* employees that increased revenues are due solely to your brilliance.

- ✗ *INFORM!* workers that the reason your revenues fell is because they're not working hard enough.

- ✗ *HIRE!* a private investigator to obtain dirt on your employees.

- ✗ *PASS!* on sex tips to make your employees more productive.

- ✗ *ALLOCATE!* and reallocate titles constantly based on a worker's contribution to the company on a particular day.

- ✗ *CRITICIZE!* employees and their supervisors during worker reviews.

- ✗ *ANNOUNCE!* bonuses in December, but pay them in June.

- ✗ *ALLOW!* good workers to chose their own pens from your show samples.

- ✗ *ARRANGE!* worker discounts at your local beauty, medical and dental colleges.

- ✗ *SCATTER!* brochures about outsourcing services throughout your organization.

- ✗ *THREATEN!* to close the company if sales staff don't sell at least $10,000 of goods in the next four hours.

- ✗ *CONSTANTLY!* praise your ex-employees.

- ✗ *WHEN!* you break a production record, complain about your workers lack of consistency.

- ✗ *GRADE!* every piece of work that your workers produce.

- ✗ *ASK!* workers if they won an award because they dated a judge or had a relative on the panel.

- ✗ *FORCE!* employees to teach their jobs to your interns.

- ✗ *EDIT!* your employees' work for as long as possible.

- ✗ *REWARD!* employees who complete their tasks early by giving them additional work to complete.

- ✗ *COMPLAIN!* about workers with foreign accents.

- ✗ *CHANGE!* workers' jobs when they get things under control.

- ✗ *QUESTION!* workers about every course of action they suggest.

- ✗ *FEEL!* free to smoke or eat when you need to work closely with an employee.

Paying Your Workers

"The worker who suffers gets everything he or she is entitled to."
—Dr. Mark Geoffrey Young

Like it or not, you have to pay your people. While feudalism was a fine system while it lasted, the days of indentured servitude and slavery are long gone. And even though you may feel that your employees are marginal workers who don't care about you or your standard of living, you still have to compensate them for their minimal efforts.

While we're all aware that the only reason your workers show up each day is because you pay them, they'll claim otherwise. While your employees may tell you that they really enjoy working for you (remember they have a hidden agenda) all they want is more of your money.

If you don't believe it, explain your life to the worker. Tell him or her that things are so tough that you're only going to Europe once this year, that your children's private school fees have gone up, or that it costs you an arm and a leg to fix your imported luxury car and see how sympathetic they are to your situation.

———•———

Commissioned salespeople always complain about the size of their commissions. Eliminate disputes by refusing to share "raw" revenue figures with them.

———•———

Prevent your workers from asking for a raise by sharing only bad news. Instead of letting your employees know when you make a large sale or acquire a new client, only provide them with news when something goes wrong or a client leaves.

———•———

Instead of offering workers unexpected bonuses, salary increases or praise when they do more than is expected, let them know that you expect this sort of effort on a regular basis.

———•———

Your company's cash flow will vary due to a number of different factors. Share this pain with your employees by letting their payroll checks bounce when things get tight.

———•———

Just because a worker does a great job doesn't mean he or she is entitled to a raise or a bonus. Instead of increasing their pay, remind them that there's more to a job than just a paycheck.

———•———

Soften up your workers for the worst by sending out newsletters in November and December highlighting the year's mistakes. This will cut your costs by reducing their expectations for bonuses and raises.

———•———

Let workers know that revenue is not an indication of profitability. Point out that because increased revenue means increased costs, you'll be unable to grant any bonuses or raises this year.

———•———

Most workers regard overtime as voluntary and expect to be paid for it. Dispel this myth by taking everybody off the clock and classifying them as "exempt" employees.

———•———

Since status is very important to workers, hand out fancy titles when you conduct salary reviews. Your employees will appreciate the fact that you've given them something to brag about with their friends over dinner.

———•———

Make your company more profitable by promoting from within whenever possible. Not only do you save money by not having to increase the affected worker's salary, you improve morale by giving the worker a new title.

———•———

Never promote from within unless you can't find an external candidate. Hiring an existing employee means you have to fill two vacancies—the promoted worker's position and the open job.

———•———

Sometimes there is no way to get around giving a worker a raise. When this occurs, increase the number of hours they're required to work by the same percentage as their raise to keep your costs under control.

———•———

Prevent your salespeople from earning too much by increasing their quota every time they reach their target. Berate them the following month if they don't hit their new numbers.

———•———

Good salespeople often earn more money that their bosses who don't receive commissions. Prevent this from happening by capping the amount of money an employee can earn.

———•———

Prevent your salespeople from working too hard by taking away their existing accounts when they get too many new clients. They'll appreciate the fact that you're looking after their interests.

———•———

When costs need to be cut, reduce the number of hours that you allocate to your part-time workers so you can hit your targets. Remember, everybody always like a little bit of extra time off.

———•———

If you're forced to eliminate part-time jobs due to economic conditions, get your remaining employees to work voluntary (and unpaid) overtime to prevent further retrenchments.

———•———

Challenge employees to reach for the sky by setting their goals so high that they can never be reached. Remind them how they failed to hit their numbers during annual reviews.

———•———

Never apologize to workers for the size of their bonus. Instead, point out how many employees only receive a base salary, and let them know that you'll move to this model if they continue to complain.

———•———

If a worker unhappy with their bonus, suggest that they take it up with their Congressman. Point out that if you didn't have to pay taxes on your profits, you'd have more money to share.

———•———

When workers complain about their salary, let them know that you have no objection to them getting a second or third job— as long as it doesn't interfere with their present responsibilities —if that's what it takes to make ends meet.

———•———

Cut the salaries of your older workers when they lose their edge. When they complain, remind them that they're not as sharp as they used to be, and how many younger workers are prepared do their job for less than their new, reduced salary.

———•———

Young employees often believe that they're worth a lot more than you pay them. Point out how many older, more experienced workers would happily do their job for a pittance of what you're currently paying them.

———•———

Feel free to share salary information when a worker asks for a raise. Instead of listening to their reasoning, simply show them how little a coworker earns, and they'll be happy with their current rate of pay.

———•———

ACTION! ITEMS

✗ *NEVER!* share "raw" revenue figures with your salespeople.

✗ *GIVE!* your employees only bad news.

✗ *RATHER!* than paying bonuses when workers perform well, let them know that you expect this effort on a regular basis.

✗ *LET!* payroll checks bounce when things get tight.

✗ *TELL!* workers there's more to a job than just a paycheck.

✗ *INFORM!* your employees that things are bad just before the holidays.

✗ *POINT!* out that increased revenues are not an indication of profitability.

✗ *ELIMINATE!* overtime by classifying all of your workers as "exempt" employees.

✗ *INSTEAD!* of raises, give your workers fancy titles.

✗ *PROMOTE!* from within to avoid costly salary increases.

✗ *NEVER!* promote from within as you have to fill two positions.

✗ *WHENEVER!* you raise a worker's salary, increase the employee's hours by the same percentage.

✗ *HIKE!* monthly quotas when your salespeople hit their targets.

✗ *CAP!* the amount of commission a salesperson can earn.

✗ *TAKE!* away a salesperson's old accounts when they acquire too many new clients.

✗ *CUT!* part-time employees' hours whenever necessary.

✗ *INTRODUCE!* voluntary and unpaid overtime after layoffs.

✗ *PREVENT!* workers from hitting their goals by constantly raising their targets.

✗ *IF!* employees complain about their bonus, tell them it's the last one they'll receive.

✗ *ADVISE!* workers that you'll increase their bonuses when they cut corporate taxes.

✗ *ENCOURAGE!* staff to get a second job to make ends meet.

✗ *REDUCE!* the salaries of older workers who aren't as sharp as they once were.

✗ *REMIND!* your younger workers that many older people earn less than they do.

✗ *SHARE!* salary information so your high-paid workers can see that they're overpaid.

SETTING HOURS AND EXPECTATIONS

"If your workers don't like you, and the going gets tough.
Tough. Get over it. You're their boss, not their friend."
—Dr. Mark Geoffrey Young

While you expect your staff to earn their salaries by working hard, your employees know that you're required to pay them just for showing up—even if they don't do anything.

The best way to prevent your workers from taking advantage of you is to watch them like a hawk. Just because an employee looks busy, doesn't mean that he or she is actually working. While you may be worried that your workers will think you don't trust them if they know they're being monitored, relax. You don't trust them. If you give your employees an inch, they'll take a mile.

In fact, your workers are already taking advantage of your niceness. If you don't believe me, ask yourself how often your people leave a few minutes early to take their allegedly sick child to a doctor, or to get a head-start on the weekend. While you may not be unduly concerned about five or ten minutes, remember, it's your time they're stealing!

But, this situation is easily to rectify—simply charge those workers who leave early a fee equal to two or three times their hourly rate for this privilege. Letting your workers know they're being monitored increases their productivity and dramatically improves your rate of return on their labor.

———•———

Home-based workers are more likely to take advantage of you than any of your other employees. Prevent this from happening by getting them to fill in on-line worksheets every fifteen minutes.

———•———

When a worker has to leave early for an emergency, say loudly "thanks for dropping in." Your employees will take advantage of you if they think you're not paying attention to their hours.

———•———

If your workers need to work late or on a weekend to meet a deadline, resist the urge to join them as your presence after hours could make them feel uncomfortable. Instead, call in frequently from your beach house to see how things are going.

———•———

Whenever a worker is late and offers an excuse, demand proof in the form of a notarized letter from the transport authority, doctor or another verifiable source.

———•———

If an employee is injured or required to perform light duties for a period of time, calculate the impact this will have on their performance and reduce their salary by this percentage.

———•——

Develop a firm but compassionate policy to deal with tardy employees. The first time the worker is late, reduce their pay by the appropriate number of minutes—then double it for each subsequent offense.

———•——

When you have to leave before a normal workday ends, call your workers from the road before their scheduled departure. If they've taken advantage of your absence and left early, deduct the appropriate amount from their salary.

———•——

Boost your productivity by calling the office while you're stuck in the morning traffic. This will allow you to talk to your workers while they're still fresh, and you'll be fully prepared the minute you enter the building.

———•——

Save money by giving your employees estimated starting and finishing times. This will give you the flexibility needed to alter a worker's the schedule when conditions change. Adjust their pay accordingly.

———•——

Offer your employees split shifts whenever possible. Workers love having time off in the middle of the day so they can run errands and recharge their batteries before returning for the evening rush.

———•——

Make friends with your workers by walking around the office and saying "good morning" to everybody at 9:00 a.m. every day. Not only will you see who made it to work on time, you'll be able to penalize those workers who are late.

————•————

Keep your sick employees in the loop by calling them frequently while they're recovering at home. Just because they can't get into the office, doesn't mean they're incapable of working from home.

————•————

Show workers how progressive you are by offering everybody flexible hours and allowing them to work at home when needed. Question their loyalty if they take you up on this offer.

————•————

Never allow employees to set their own hours. Instead set "core" hours, say 8:00 a.m. to 5:00 p.m., when everybody is required to be at work. Allow workers to spend additional time in the office when it's required.

————•————

Get the home phone numbers of your workers in different time zones so you can contact them whenever an emergency arises. Having to wait until the following day could dramatically reduce your productivity.

————•————

Stop your employees from leaving early by walking through the halls every day between 4:30 p.m. and 5:30 p.m. While this may appear to be a waste of time, it's more productive than allowing your workers to leave early.

————•————

Because many factors can determine how many workers are needed on a weekend, decide which employees will work at

4:30 p.m. on Friday. Staff who are not needed will appreciate the time off.

———•———

Improve your productivity by requiring workers to clock out whenever they take a cigarette break. Not only will they spend longer at their desks if they know they're being monitored, they'll thank you for reducing their cigarette bill.

———•———

Although family sizes are shrinking, workers seem to have more relatives than ever. Prevent your employees from "inventing" family and taking unneccessary personal days by demanding a notarized death certificate when they claim they're attending a funeral.

———•———

If you're forced to close early due to a power failure, unfavorable weather conditions or an emergency, give your workers the opportunity to make up the lost hours by working late the following day.

———•———

When employees work overtime or come in on a weekend, remind them that they're professionals and that you expect them to do what it takes to get the job done.

———•———

Funerals are a time of sadness for everybody concerned. Show your compassion by giving the affected worker time off to attend the event. Remind them that it's not an all-day occasion and that you expect them in the office before and after the event.

———•———

Get the news from your traveling workers quickly by requiring everybody to return to the office immediately after their flight lands. If it's a redeye or night flight, give them till 9:00 a.m. the next day to prepare their report.

———•———

Show your workers how much you value their services by placing them on call for the weekends that fall on each side of their vacation.

———•———

Inform employees that their vacation starts after the office closes—not twenty or thirty minutes before their normal workday ends. Prevent them from stealing your time by assigning them a last-minute project to complete before they depart.

———•———

ACTION! ITEMS

- ✗ *GET!* home-based workers to fill in on-line time sheets every fifteen minutes.

- ✗ *RESIST!* the urge to join your staff in the office after hours.

- ✗ *CHASTISE!* workers who leave early for their lack of commitment to the company.

- ✗ *DEMAND!* proof whenever a worker gives you an excuse for arriving late.

- ✗ *REDUCE!* workers' pay if they're injured on the job and placed on light duties.

- ✗ *DOCK!* workers' salaries when they're late. Double the penalty for each subsequent offence.

- ✗ *CALL!* the office for updates when you leave early.

- ✗ *PHONE!* the office during the morning rush so you can be fully prepared when you arrive.

- ✗ *GIVE!* workers estimated started and finishing times.

- ✗ *OFFER!* split shifts so workers can attend to personal matters.

- ✗ *WALK!* around the office at 9:00 a.m. to see who is late.

- ✗ *CALL!* sick workers at home several times a day.

- ✗ *OFFER!* flexible hours only as a gesture.

- ✗ *SET!* core hours, but allow workers to put in additional time when it's needed.

- ✗ *TELEPHONE!* your employees at home at anytime of the day or night.

- ✗ *WALK!* the halls after 4:30 p.m. to prevent your employees from leaving early.

✗ *DETERMINE!* how many weekend employees you will need at 4:30 p.m. on Fridays.

✗ *HAVE!* workers clock out each time they take a break.

✗ *INSIST!* that workers present notarized death certificates when they attend a funeral.

✗ *PERMIT!* workers to make up the time they lost during a power failure or snow storm.

✗ *INFORM!* workers that they're professionals and there's no such thing as paid overtime.

✗ *GIVE!* workers time off for funerals, but tell them to turn up before and after the event.

✗ *REMIND!* employees on the redeye that they're still expected in the office by 9:00 a.m.

✗ *PLACE!* workers on call during the weekends before and after their vacation.

✗ *INFORM!* employees that they're not permitted to leave early for their vacation.

Granting Vacations

"The purpose of your life is not to make your workers happy,
it's to use your workers to make you rich."
—Dr. Mark Geoffrey Young

Even though you must pay your workers who show up at the office—whether or not they actually do anything—you're going to be even more surprised to find out that you also have to give everyone a week or two's vacation every year. And, to add insult to injury, you're required to pay them for this time.

That's right, the old motto of "an honest day's pay for an honest day's work" now reads "an honest day's pay for not much work." While there's nothing you can do about this, you don't have to take the situation lying down.

Instead of just giving your employees time off, force them to earn their vacations by working extra hours to compensate for the time they'll be out of the office. Get them to call in two or three times a day while they're away to deal with their day-to-day responsibilities. Remember, even though you're required to give your employees time off, there's no law that prevents them from working while they're on vacation.

———•———

When an employee goes on vacation, use the opportunity to clean your offices. Since not everything you collect is garbage, place all of the items you've collected in their cubicle so they can go through it when they return.

———•———

Show your workers know how valuable they are by constantly rescheduling their vacation to a time that's more convenient for the company.

———•———

Booking last minute vacations is both difficult and expensive. Give your workers plenty of notice by posting the vacation schedule in January. Show how flexible you are by allowing them to make changes with six months notice.

———•———

Reduce the pressure that vacationing workers place on their coworkers by only allowing your employees to take only one week off at a time—regardless of the circumstances.

———•———

Inform your workers that elective surgery is a self-induced illness (like a hangover) that doesn't qualify as sick time. Tell them if they want to be paid, they must use their vacation time.

———•———

Encourage your workers to increase their knowledge of your industry by sending them to seminars and trade shows during their vacation. Make it cost-effective for the employee by offering to split the cost of the hotel with them.

———·———

Prevent your clients and other workers from suffering when an employee takes a vacation by ensuring that everybody has the vacationing worker's cell phone number. If your employee objects, remind him or her that it only takes a few minutes to return a call.

———·———

Call your employees while they're on vacation a couple of times a day to keep them up to date with what's happening in the office. While this may appear intrusive, it saves time when they return to work.

———·———

Reduce the stresses of business travel on your employees by allowing them to visit clients while they're on vacation. They'll thank you when they return for not having to spend time away from their family.

———·———

Allow workers to buy additional vacation time during slow periods. Charge them a fifty percent premium on their normal salary to compensate for the additional stresses their absence places on your other employees.

———·———

Let your vacationing employees know that even though they're not in the office, they're still being paid. Remind them that they must respond to email and voicemail at least twice a day.

———·———

ACTION! ITEMS

- ✗ *SCHEDULE!* an office cleanup and store these items in a vacationing worker's office.

- ✗ *SHOW!* workers how valuable they are by constantly rescheduling their vacations.

- ✗ *ALLOW!* workers to change their vacation dates with six months notice.

- ✗ *NEVER!* allow your workers take more than one week's vacation at a time.

- ✗ *TELL!* workers that elective surgery must be scheduled during their vacation.

- ✗ *ENCOURAGE!* your workers to attend seminars and trade shows during their vacation.

- ✗ *GET!* employees to give their cell phone number to clients and coworkers before they leave before they leave for vacation.

- ✗ *CALL!* workers constantly while they're on vacation to keep them in the loop.

- ✗ *REDUCE!* travel expenses by allowing workers to visit clients during their vacation.

- ✗ *SELL!* workers additional vacation time during slow periods.

- ✗ *REMIND!* employees that they must respond to email and phone calls while they're on vacation.

MANAGING YOUR WORKERS

"People who are able to demotivate others will find it easy to achieve greatness."
—Dr. Mark Geoffrey Young

Even though you allow your workers to take it easy when they're on vacation, you must let them know that they're required to work to their fullest while they're in the office. If you fail to make this clear, your employees will take advantage of your generous nature and waste your time by instant messaging their friends, talking to their family and running errands when they're supposed to be working.

If you think your workers are dedicated, think again. No matter how good you think your employees are, or how hard they appear to work, the sad fact of the matter is that every worker will take advantage of you if you give them the opportunity. To prevent this from happening, you need to constantly point them in the right direction.

If you leave your employees to their own devices, they'll find the easiest way to do their job and rush out the door at the first opportunity. While you may not begrudge your employees a happy home life, remember, their only purpose is to make your job easier.

———•———

Show your staff that they're part of your team by giving everyone a nickname. Baldy, Skinny, Tiny, Shorty and Fatty are good starting points.

———•———

Even if you remember a worker's name, never use it. "Hey you," should be sufficient. To be an effective manager you need to distinguish yourself from the workers.

———•———

Keep your office door closed whenever possible. Not only does this prevent interruptions, it shows your workers how important you are. Since nobody walks in to the President's or Prime Minister's office unannounced, keeping your door shut places you in the same league.

———•———

Reduce the temptation for your employees to goof off and improve their productivity by eliminating all distractions. Blacking out all of the windows in your office is one idea.

———•———

Instead of seating your workers in the department where they work, organize seating based on attractiveness. Placing your beautiful staff members in the front where your clients can see them, creates a better first impression. Rearrange the seating every time you hire a new employee.

———•———

Spend a lot of time with your employees discussing how every change will affect your organization. Look at every minute detail, regardless of how small it appears, to ensure that you're fully prepared.

———•———

Don't waste time explaining how your changes will impact your workers' jobs. Letting your employees know what you're planning will cost you money as they'll waste time complaining about the impact to their coworkers.

———•———

If an employee comes up with an idea, maintain the status quo for as long as possible. Making changes quickly causes problems because your workers are used to doing things a certain way.

———•———

Whenever a worker speaks with you, question him or her thoroughly about their motives. No matter how logical their point of view may appear—remember, every employee has a hidden agenda. Taking what they say at face value always costs you money.

———•———

Encourage your workers to multi-task by getting them to work on several projects simultaneously—each with a different boss. This not only helps them obtain skills in a variety of areas, it allows your employees to receive feedback from managers in different sections.

———•———

Keep your workers on the ball by tossing paper clips and other items at them as you pass their desk. This is especially effective with employees who appear to have had a hard night or are recovering from an illness.

———·———

Give every worker a target and quota that's impossible to reach and chastise those who fail to hit that number. If you make your targets achievable, your workers will cease working the moment they hit the goal.

———·———

Let your employees know that you're superior to them by refusing to help clean up or carry equipment to distant locations. Feel free to complain about how much you're paying them or how slowly they're working.

———·———

Reduce your stress levels by delegating whenever possible. Allowing your workers to handle all of the mundane tasks ensures that you make the best possible use of your time.

———·———

Ensure that everything meets your standards by signing off on everything—no matter how menial it may appear—while simultaneously complaining about how busy you are. Delegating tasks always causes problems.

———·———

Improve your productivity by eliminating the need for your workers to think. By over-specifying everything you want done, you allow your workers to spend their time doing their job, instead of thinking about it.

———·———

Give your workers a feeling of ownership by allowing them to determine the best way to do their jobs. Offering guidance and suggestions turns your skilled employees into mere assistants.

———•———

Encourage your workers to come up with creative and innovative ways to do their jobs. Setting clear expectations, targets and goals costs you money as your employees will do things they way they've always been done.

———•———

Issue every worker with a defined job contract and berate those workers who take on additional responsibilities. Your other employees will be offended if someone else attempts to do their job.

———•———

Encourage your workers to expand their horizons by tackling tasks that are outside their area of expertise. Allowing employees to share their skills and expertise with your other workers ensures that everybody benefits.

———•———

Never allow workers to set their own deadlines or tell you how long a job will take to complete. Letting employees set their own targets shows that you're a weak leader and this will cause them to question your authority.

———•———

If you hear laughter or talking in a hallway, rush out and berate your workers. Tell them that you run a workplace—not a comedy club—and if they've run out of things to do, you have additional work available.

———•———

To encourage learning, get your workers to print out all their documents and walk them over to you for review. Making your comments directly onto their printouts ensures that your workers learn from their mistakes by forcing them to input your changes manually.

——•——

Bond with your workers and let them know that you have a sense of humor by offering to share your jokes with them as soon as the workday is over.

——•——

Assign new employees a mentor to make it easier for them to fit into the company. To keep costs down, make sure the mentor is on a business trip for the new worker's first couple of weeks.

——•——

Because all good ideas come from management, never ask employees for ideas. If by chance you do get a good suggestion, pass it off as your own.

——•——

Insist that workers keep the windows closed when the air conditioning fails to reduce the chance of bugs getting into the computers.

——•——

ACTION! ITEMS

✗ *GIVE!* every worker a nickname.

✗ *SEPARATE!* management and workers by never using an employee's name.

✗ *KEEP!* your office door closed at all times.

✗ *BLACK!* out all of the office windows to reduce distractions.

✗ *SEAT!* your workers based on their attractiveness.

✗ *SPEND!* a lot of time discussing how changes will impact your company.

✗ *DON'T!* waste time explaining how changes will affect your organization.

✗ *REJECT!* or delay all changes suggested by your employees.

✗ *QUESTION!* employees on their motives every time they speak with you.

✗ *ENCOURAGE!* workers to multi-task by giving them several projects with different bosses.

✗ *TOSS!* paperclips and other items at workers to keep them on their toes.

✗ *SET!* unachievable goals and chastise employees who don't reach them.

✗ *REFUSE!* to clean up or carry equipment to distant locations.

✗ *DELEGATE!* projects after the challenging parts are completed.

✗ *SIGN!* off on every task regardless of how menial or insignificant it appears.

✗ *OVER!* specify everything you want to reduce the chance of errors occurring.

- ✗ *ENCOURAGE!* your workers to think by refusing to give guidance or clear directions.

- ✗ *DO!* not set clear expectations, targets or goals.

- ✗ *YELL!* at workers who tackle tasks that aren't explicitly stated in their job description.

- ✗ *GET!* workers to acquire new skills and expand their knowledge by performing work in new areas.

- ✗ *IMPROVE!* productivity by refusing to allow workers to set their own deadlines.

- ✗ *TELL!* employees who are talking or laughing that you have extra work available.

- ✗ *EDUCATE!* workers by making changes on paper instead of directly into the digital document.

- ✗ *SHARE!* your sense of humor with your workers after the workday is complete.

- ✗ *ASSIGN!* new workers a mentor who's on vacation.

- ✗ *PASS!* off all good ideas submitted by workers as your own.

- ✗ *INSIST!* that workers keep the windows shut to reduce the chance of bugs getting into the computers.

DEALING WITH YOUR CUSTOMERS

"We don't want ideas from our customers, we simply want them to buy what we make."—Dr. Mark Geoffrey Young

No matter how often you tell your staff that they're not permitted to give away anything for free, they'll do anything they can do to encourage a potential customer to purchase additional products and services. While this will increase their commission, giveaways cut into your bottom line. The only way you can prevent this from happening is to monitor every customer interaction—and since you're far too busy to deal with clients, you're going to have to delegate customer service.

And, no matter how much time you spend training your workers or how specific your instructions are, your employees are going to screw up and upset your customers. When this happens, the best thing to do is to keep your nose clean and stay as far away from the situation as possible. Remember, you're paying your workers to make your life easier. Make them earn their money.

By making yourself unapproachable, you not only have more time to deal with the issues of concern, you place your customers on the same pedestal as your workers—people who should be avoided whenever possible.

By refusing to get involved in customer disputes, you'll reduce your stress levels and allow your workers to take the heat. And, when you do get involved, it's much easier to rectify the situation—you simply fire the worker and replace him or her with a cheaper employee.

———•———

Keep your reputation intact by getting your workers to call a customer when you miss a deadline. Using the old excuse that it's better to get something late that's right, than to get it on time and have it wrong makes the customer feel better.

———•———

If there's no way to meet the deadline, deliver the parts of the job that you've completed. Tell your workers to blame the warehouse and have them inform the client that the boss is looking into it.

———•———

Inspire creativity in your workers by refusing to issue credits or refunds. They'll enjoy the challenge of appeasing unhappy customers when they can't take the easy and obvious route to client satisfaction.

———•———

Get your workers to treat the company's money like their own by deducting all refunds and credits from their paychecks.

———•———

When a customer brings back an item that you can't return to the manufacturer, get a worker to shrink wrap it and place it back on the shelf. The chances of it coming back a second time are very small.

———•———

If a product is out of stock, get your workers to tell your customers that it's in short supply, but you do have a limited quantity arriving tomorrow. Getting a non-refundable deposit improves your cash flow and allows you to earn interest on the client's money while you wait for the item to arrive.

———•———

Help your workers learn how valuable their time is by forcing them to resolve all customer complaints in less than three minutes. Penalize employees for every interaction that exceeds this time.

———•———

Cash in on the fact that tall people are more credible by insisting that all of your employees wear six-inch platform shoes. You'll also reduce the number of complaints you receive, because customers will be too afraid to argue with people who scare them.

———•———

Keep your workers on their toes by sharing every piece of negative customer feedback that comes into your organization. Let them know that if things don't improve, you'll be forced to fire everybody.

———•———

Never share customer compliments with your employees. Letting your workers know that they're doing something right takes the pressure off and encourages them to take it easy.

———•———

Forbid your employees from asking your customers for input about your products and services. Giving clients the opportunity to express their opinions is asking for trouble—if they weren't satisfied, they'd go elsewhere.

———•———

Make your company seem bigger than it is by creating an impressive front lobby and waiting room for your clients. Your staff will happily put up with cramped conditions if they know your customers are happy.

———•———

Generate extra income by hiring workers who speak other languages so you can expand your business into new communities. To encourage a feeling of belonging, insist that all employee communications take place in English.

———•———

Show respect for your customers by refusing to allow your staff to use the customer facilities—even when the staff bathrooms are out of order.

———•———

Forward all your calls to voicemail. To show your customers how important you are, get your workers to call them back. Anybody who really wants to speak to you will call again.

———•———

Have your staff generate extra income by billing clients for any extra services such as using your office phone or providing them with food or beverages during a meeting.

———•———

Increase your revenues by insisting that your staff charge sales tax to all your customers—even those who live out of state. If a customer complains, blame a worker and promise to refund the overcharged amount. Most clients will never check their statements to see if you followed through.

———•———

Since most of your workers can't add, make their life easier by having your cash registers and accounting programs automatically round up all your prices to the nearest dollar. Apologize and blame your workers if a customer complains.

———•———

To stop your bar employees giving away your profits, measure how much alcohol is on the premises when they start their shift, and how much is left when they finish. Deduct any discrepancies from their paycheck.

———•———

ACTION! ITEMS

✗ *GET!* your staff to pass on all bad news to customers.

✗ *WHEN!* you miss a deadline, deliver the parts you have and blame the warehouse for the screwup.

✗ *HAVE!* your staff explain why they can't issue a refund.

✗ *DEDUCT!* all credits and refunds from workers' paychecks.

✗ *PLACE!* items that can't be returned back on the shelf.

✗ *ACCEPT!* deposits for out-of-stock items and promise next-day delivery.

✗ *FINE!* workers who take over three minutes to handle inquiries.

✗ *MAKE!* your staff more credible by having them wear tall shoes.

✗ *SHARE!* negative feedback with your workers.

✗ *DON'T!* pass along customer compliments to your staff.

✗ *DO!* not ask your customers for input.

✗ *ALLOW!* only English to be spoken in your organization.

✗ *CREATE!* a large waiting area to make your company seem larger than it really is.

✗ *NEVER!* allow your workers to use the customer facilities.

✗ *INSIST!* that your workers return all of your phone calls.

✗ *BILL!* your customers for using your phone.

✗ *CHARGE!* sales tax on all out-of-state orders.

✗ *ROUND!* up all charges at the cash register and on your bills.

✗ *DEDUCT!* any liquor shortages from your employees' salaries.

Making Your Company More Profitable

"If you don't tell your workers where to go, they'll never end up in the right place."—Dr. Mark Geoffrey Young

Most business owners realize that having happy, satisfied customers who pay for everything is essential if they're going to make money, however, very few bosses view their workers as potential clients.

Instead of seeing your employees as a drain on your profits, view them as a huge, untapped revenue opportunity. Even though your workers may not be potential clients for your products, you can increase your revenues by charging them for the services you now provide free.

While many companies install vending machines and pay phones for their workers' convenience, these can be a significant income source if you price the products correctly. Another way to increase your profits is to eliminate non-essential luxuries such as hot water, coffee and outlets that allows employees to charge a cell phone or iPod.

You can also improve your profits by cutting back on staff. Offering unpaid internships not only gives the leaders of tomorrow a chance to get experience and improve their self esteem, it also improves your profits and standing in the community. While you may be concerned about how your employees will react, remember, your workers show up only because they need a job, not because they like you.

———•———

Even though telephone calls are cheaper than ever, you still have to pay for them. A simple way to reduce your costs is to get two or three workers to share a phone.

———•———

Reduce your phone costs by placing a jar next to each telephone. Making it easy for your workers to pay for their personal calls—and playing with their conscience—dramatically increases your ancillary income.

———•———

Improve productivity by insisting that your workers remove their jackets and coats before they enter the office. Having everyone ready to work the minute they reach their desks, dramatically reduces the amount of time your employees can steal from you.

———•———

Prevent your restaurant workers from giving away too-large portions by calculating exactly how many people you can feed with the food you purchased. Charge your employees if they the food doesn't stretch as far as you expect.

———•———

Use family members wherever possible. This not only ensures an endless supply of cheap labor, it keeps your employees on their toes by showing them how easy they are to replace.

———•———

Reduce your healthcare costs by choosing a health plan with a high deductible. You don't want your workers rushing to the doctor every time they have a headache.

———•———

If a worker breaks or damages something that belongs to the company, deduct the item's full retail cost from their next paycheck. After all, you did have to buy it.

———•———

When a piece of equipment breaks, replace it with a device that's older than the one that failed. This encourages workers to respect company property.

———•———

Remove every second light bulb to reduce your electricity costs. This also saves you money because you only have to replace half as many bulbs when they burn out.

———•———

Teach your workers the value of a dollar and increase your profits by charging them the full cost of their health insurance, disability and unemployment. While you may want to be a benevolent employer, remember, workers don't appreciate things unless they're forced to pay for them themselves.

———•———

Improve your profitability by giving workers their own telephone code for calls that can't be charged to a client. At the end of each month, deduct the cost of personal calls from their salary.

——•——

Deduct a security deposit from an employee's first paycheck to cover the cost of their company ID, keys, uniforms and other property. Return this upon termination if all property is returned in its original, pristine condition.

——•——

Reduce costs, conserve paper and do your part to save the environment by using six-point type for all employee contracts and other documents that have little value.

——•——

Encourage your workers to follow the law by making them pay for any workplace violations or fines that occur on their shift.

——•——

Hire a temp and get him or her to learn everybody's job. This not only allows workers see their true value—it show them how easy they are to replace.

——•——

Make your employees work harder by refusing to hire temporary workers during peak periods. If an employee complains, remind him or her that their predecessors were able to do the job without help.

——•——

Get your staff to work harder by hiring everybody on a temporary basis when they start. Tell them you'll make them permanent as soon as they prove their worth.

——•——

Private offices reduce productivity, create isolation and increase costs by forcing businesses to rent more space than needed. Increase productivity, improve worker satisfaction and reduce costs by replacing offices with cubicles.

———•———

Discourage unqualified workers from applying for jobs at your company by charging potential employees a fee to cover fingerprinting, background checks and administrative costs.

———•———

Reduce costs by refusing to order items until you're completely out. Employees have their own unique ways of coping during shortages, including bringing in their own supplies from home.

———•———

To see if a new worker has what it takes to survive in your company, wait at least six months after he or she starts to order supplies such as business cards.

———•———

Remember that everything in the company belongs to you. As such, don't feel obliged to return pens or other items that you "borrow" from your workers.

———•———

Place your children and other relatives in charge of as many divisions as possible—regardless of their age or qualifications. Not only will you reduce your costs, you'll also get the lowdown on everything that's happening.

———•———

Follow the law to the letter by never giving workers more than is required. Offering time off and bonuses causes friction with your other workers and leads to a feeling of entitlement.

———•———

Keep salary increases to a minimum by turning your skilled workers into your assistants. When it comes to review time, you can honestly point out that they're not doing the jobs they were hired to do.

———•———

Install a pay phone for personal calls. This not only improves your bottom line, it also improves productivity by keeping calls to less than three minutes.

———•———

Boost your profits and get your salespeople to choose their clients carefully by deducting any unpaid invoices from their salaries.

———•———

Charge employees who lose or damage their company ID, keys or other property the full replacement cost, as well as an administrative fee so they'll be more careful in the future.

———•———

Teach workers the value of the Earth's finite resources by fining employees who leave the lights on when they leave the room, or allow heat or air conditioning to escape through an open door or window.

———•———

Issue workers a set amount of office supplies each month. Charge those who exceed their quota a fee for each additional pen, piece of paper or envelope that they use.

———•———

Encourage your employees to use public transportation and conserve gas by charging them a fee to use your parking lot.

———•———

ACTION! ITEMS

- ✗ *CUT!* your telephone charges by getting your employees to share a telephone.

- ✗ *PLACE!* a jar next to each phone to recoup the charges.

- ✗ *DEMAND!* that workers remove their coats before they enter the premises.

- ✗ *INSIST!* that your employees pay for any food shortages.

- ✗ *USE!* family members whenever possible.

- ✗ *KEEP!* your healthcare costs down by choosing a plan with a high deductible.

- ✗ *MAKE!* your workers pay for any equipment they break.

- ✗ *REPLACE!* equipment that breaks with an older model.

- ✗ *REMOVE!* every second light bulb.

- ✗ *IMPROVE!* profitability by giving workers a code and charging them for personal phone calls.

- ✗ *REQUIRE!* every employee to pay a security deposit for their IDs, keys and uniforms.

- ✗ *USE!* six-point type for employee contracts.

- ✗ *HAVE!* your workers pay for any violations or fines that occur on their shift.

- ✗ *TEACH!* every worker's job to a temporary worker.

- ✗ *NEVER!* hire temps to handle peak loads.

- ✗ *HIRE!* everybody as a temporary worker.

- ✗ *REMOVE!* all of your employees' private offices and replace them with very small cubicles.

- ✗ *COVER!* your hiring costs by charging potential employees an application fee.

- ✗ *ONLY!* purchase office supplies when you're out of everything.

- ✗ *ORDER!* business cards only after the employee has proved him or herself.

- ✗ *DON'T!* return items you borrow.

- ✗ *PLACE!* your children and relatives in charge of divisions.

- ✗ *PROVIDE!* workers only with what is required by law.

- ✗ *ELIMINATE!* salary increases by turning your skilled employees into your assistants.

- ✗ *INSTALL!* a pay phone for your workers' personal calls.

- ✗ *BILL!* salespeople the full amount of any unpaid invoices.

- ✗ *GET!* workers who lose company property to pay the full cost plus an administrative fee.

- ✗ *FINE!* employees who leave the lights on.

- ✗ *ISSUE!* workers who exceed their office supply quota with an invoice for the items they've used.

- ✗ *CHARGE!* employees who park their cars in the company lot a fee for their space.

RECOGNIZING YOUR WORKERS

"Awards are meaningful to everybody. I encourage all employees to actively campaign for one."—Dr. Mark Geoffrey Young

Even though you only employ workers to increase your profits and perform the tasks that are beneath you, it's a good idea to occasionally recognize those employees who go "above and beyond" what's required. While most bosses are concerned about the cost, advances in computer technology now make it possible to produce impressive looking certificates for less than a dime.

And, believe it or not, awards are more effective at boosting productivity than salary increases. Why? Workers are simple creatures who crave recognition. If you give it to them, they'll continue toiling long and hard for a lot less money than it would otherwise cost you. Use this knowledge to improve your profitability. Instead of giving a worker a bonus for landing a big account, give them a certificate to display in their cubicle.

It's not just salespeople who seek recognition. If you want to inspire your other employees, place an honor board in your reception area and come up with a reason to make someone the "Employee of the Month," and that person will put in 110 percent the following month. When used properly, awards can add thousands of dollars to your bottom line each year.

———•———

Reward your workers for a job well done by presenting them with discount certificates for other businesses in your area. Not only will many firms give you the certificates for free, they'll thank you for driving extra business their way.

———•———

Recognize those employees who perform well by giving them additional work and responsibilities. This not only shows how pleased you are with a worker's performance, it also lets you replace higher-paid employees with lower-paid workers who will work harder to prove themselves.

———•———

Encourage your workers to undertake both short courses and advanced degrees in their spare time. Let them know that while you're unable to contribute to the cost, it will be noted on their permanent record.

———•———

Designate a parking space near the door for the Employee of the Month. Make the worker feel loved by getting him or her to run special errands for you.

———•———

Instead of promoting workers, give them an acting title. You'll save money and the employee will get the experience they need to advance their career. It's a win-win situation for everybody.

———•———

Reduce costs by encouraging your workers to come up with money-saving ideas. Show your appreciation by selling them merchandise with the company logo at slightly above cost.

———•———

Build the company spirit and recognize those workers who do what's required by getting everybody to compete for a single bonus called a "reward."

———•———

When a worker finally gets a degree or qualification, keep his or her ego in check by explaining that you expect them to make fewer mistakes now that they're educated.

———•———

After a worker completes a course, let him or her know that you expect them to spend more time working as they no longer have to waste time traveling to and from school.

———•———

Prevent your over-ambitious employees from getting big heads by transferring them to another job just before they complete a project. This keeps their egos under control and reduces the amount you have to pay out in bonuses.

———•———

ACTION! ITEMS

- ✗ *PRESENT!* employees who perform well with discount certificates for other local businesses.

- ✗ *REWARD!* workers who do well by giving them extra work and responsibilities.

- ✗ *ENCOURAGE!* employees to study on their own time.

- ✗ *PROVIDE!* the Employee of the Month with a parking near the door so he or she can run your errands quickly.

- ✗ *GIVE!* staff an acting title instead of promoting them.

- ✗ *SELL!* staff who reduce expenses items with the company logo at slightly above cost.

- ✗ *GET!* your employees to compete for a single bonus called a reward.

- ✗ *INFORM!* workers who get a degree that you expect fewer mistakes now that they're educated.

- ✗ *TELL!* employees who get a degree that you expect them to work longer now that they've finished school.

- ✗ *KEEP!* your employees' egos under control by transferring them before a project is complete.

Keeping Your Workers in Line

"The workers who fail are those who don't follow the instructions they are given."
—Dr. Mark Geoffrey Young

While it's important to recognize your workers' achievements if you want them to continue toiling for you at their present salaries, it's even more vital to remind them that your word is law. If you allow your employees to forget this, they'll see it as a sign of weakness and question your every decision.

This would be disastrous. Not only would you lose your infallible status, your workers would expect to be included in the decision-making process. Imagine trying to run an organization where your employees believe that you care about them, that their jobs matter and that they can influence your organization's future direction.

Prevent this from happening by insisting that your employees do their jobs in the exact manner prescribed. If workers question your logic, ignore them. Remember, you're not required to respond—or even acknowledge their presence.

———•———

Stop your workers from waiting until the last minute to complete their tasks by responding to urgent emails when you have time. This will ensure they allow enough time in the future to get your input.

———•———

Even though you may not be starting a project for some time, send out an urgent email requesting information at the first opportunity. This ensures that you'll have everything you need to begin the task when you're ready.

———•———

Show your employees that you can relate to the common people by complaining about how lazy your butler, chauffeur, nanny, pilot and landscape artist are.

———•———

Maintain your office hierarchy and prevent your staff from mixing with your customers by only allowing them to enter and exit your premises only through the rear doors.

———•———

When you see an employee working on a project that they're enjoying, reassign it to another worker. If your employees start to have fun, they're not really working.

———•———

Show your workers how much you value their services by using paper nameplates on offices and cubicles.

———•———

When workers complain about unrealistic deadlines, let them know if they can't meet them, you'll find employees who can.

———•———

Complain loudly to your workers that they're not doing their jobs if the competition comes up with an idea before you do. Fire the responsible party to encourage your remaining staff to keep on eye on your competitors in the future.

———•———

Don't waste time talking about your competitors. Your workers will function much better if they only have to concern themselves with your products.

———•———

Remind staff that your clients are the reason your company exists. Endorse their products with unprecedented zeal—regardless of their overall quality, price or usefulness.

———•———

Workers love stories about how things used to be done. When you have time, explain how you used to work through weekends without sleep—and still manage to get to work early on Monday mornings.

———•———

Prevent workers from taking advantage of you by disregarding all of their estimates about how long a project will take to complete. Instead, impose your own schedule—employees always add extra time to a project to reduce their stress levels.

———•———

If a worker has a clean desk, assign him or her additional work, as they're not working to capacity. If they have time to clean their desk, they have time to complete additional tasks.

———•———

Berate workers with messy desks—it's an indication that they don't care about the image they're projecting. Let them know that good workers think nothing of spending a few extra minutes at the end of each day cleaning up after themselves.

———•———

Show your skill at managing your overseas employees by getting them to do everything exactly the same way it's done at the head office—regardless of local conditions, laws or customs.

———•———

Let your workers know that researching projects on the Internet should be conducted on their own time.

———•———

Prevent employees from abusing your Internet connection by monitoring usage. At the end of each week, produce a log and get them to justify every site they visited.

———•———

Allocate employee parking spaces based on a worker's value to the firm. Reallocate these spaces daily to prevent workers from becoming complacent.

———•———

Help your employees stay in shape by placing staff parking spaces as far away from your building as possible. Your workers will get exercise and save money as they'll no longer need hire a personal trainer.

———•———

Employees have a lot of clothes they never wear. Encourage them to show them off these items by keeping the temperature at 50 degrees during winter and at 95 degrees in summer. Your employees may even use this idea at home.

———•———

If one of your workers is sailing along without any problems, drop by their desk to find out what they're hiding from you. If they think they can get something past you, they will.

———•———

Show a genuine interest in your workers by asking them about their families. Don't feel bad if you walk away midway through a sentence—just asking shows that you care.

———•———

Having a knowledgeable workforce is essential if you're going to compete in today's marketplace. Test your employees frequently on current events and industry happenings to ensure that they're on the ball.

———•———

To keep morale in your company high, never confront a worker who does something wrong. Instead, discuss the problem with your other employees to ensure that the message gets back to him or her.

———•———

Whenever you have a bad day or something goes wrong, call the nearest worker into your office and take it out on him or her. Your employees have to learn when to approach you.

———•———

Every time a worker enters your office, let them know how important he or she is by checking your email and voicemail while they talk.

———•———

Let your workers know how valuable your time is by making them wait every time they come to see you—even if they have an appointment.

———•———

Improve communication within your company by leaving constructive voicemails on your workers' phones after they've left for the day. Feel free to raise your voice and display your emotions so they'll know exactly how you feel.

———•———

Complain constantly that your employees are not putting in enough hours and that you're going broke—regardless of how many hours they're actually working.

———•———

Let your employees know that the office is to be used only for work by refusing to allow any onsite activities such as yoga to take place during their lunch break.

———•———

ACTION! ITEMS

✗ *RESPOND!* to urgent emails when you have time.

✗ *MAKE!* every request urgent—regardless of when you actually need the information.

✗ *COMPLAIN!* about your butler, chauffeur, nanny, pilot and landscape artist constantly to your workers.

✗ *ONLY!* allow workers to enter through the rear doors.

✗ *REASSIGN!* the project if a worker appears to be enjoying it.

✗ *SHOW!* workers their true value by using paper nameplates.

✗ *REJECT!* all worker comments regarding unrealistic deadlines.

✗ *FIRE!* workers if the competition comes up with an idea or product before you do.

✗ *DON'T!* waste time talking about your competitors.

✗ *PUSH!* all of your clients' products, regardless of their quality or usefulness.

✗ *TALK!* to your workers about how things used to be done.

✗ *NEVER!* ask a worker how long a project will take to complete.

✗ *GIVE!* staff with clean desks extra work to complete.

✗ *BERATE!* workers with messy desks for not caring about the image they're projecting.

✗ *GET!* every office to follow procedures set by HQ regardless of local customs or laws.

✗ *INFORM!* employees that surfing the Internet for information is fun, not research.

- ✗ MONITOR! Internet usage and get employees to justify every site they've visited.

- ✗ REALLOCATE! parking spaces based on a worker's value to your organization each day.

- ✗ IMPLEMENT! a fitness program by forcing your employees to park far away from the office.

- ✗ ENCOURAGE! employees to wear all their clothes by eliminating heating and air conditioning.

- ✗ WHEN! things appear to be going well, find out what your workers are hiding from you.

- ✗ TUNE! out midway through a worker's conversation.

- ✗ TEST! your employees daily on current events and their general industry knowledge.

- ✗ PREVENT! misunderstandings by never confronting your employees directly.

- ✗ TAKE! out all your frustrations on your workers.

- ✗ CHECK! email and voicemail while you speak with workers.

- ✗ FORCE! your workers to wait every time they come to see you.

- ✗ LEAVE! constructive voicemails on your employees' phones after hours.

- ✗ COMPLAIN! that your employees are not working enough hours.

- ✗ REFUSE! to allow your office to be used for any non-work activities.

THE BATHROOM RULES

"The length of a one-minute bathroom break depends on whether an employee is on their time, or company time."– Dr. Mark Geoffrey Young

Another place where you need to "monitor" your employees is the bathroom. Most companies fail to realize how much it costs to provide these facilities—or how their workers abuse them. For example, whenever an employee decides that life is too hard, or that they just need some time to themselves, they race off to the bathroom for some peace and quiet.

Back in the old days, farm laborers thought nothing of walking half a mile to use the facilities after they finished an honest day's work. And, they did their business as quickly as possible because not only were the facilities less than impressive, they didn't get paid to sit and think like today's workers.

While those days aren't coming back, you can reduce the amount of time your workers spend in the bathroom by instituting policies that discourage its use. Yes, your workers will scream, but they'll eventually simmer down and make the best of the situation.

—·—

Prevent your workers from wasting time in the bathroom by following them into the facilities and asking them questions as they do their business.

—·—

Improve your profitability and make your company more efficient by giving every employee a set number of minutes to use the bathroom each day. Fine those who exceed their allocation.

—·—

Have IT create a spreadsheet that lets you record how many times an employee visits the bathroom, and how long they spend in the facilities. Penalize those who waste too much time.

—·—

Since locating employees is sometimes difficult, don't hesitate to catch them just before they enter the bathroom. Because your workers know how valuable your time is, they'll spend as long as necessary discussing whatever is on your mind.

—·—

Get the most out of your workers by allocating each of them a specific time to use the facilities. If they complain, remind them how they managed to do their business between classes when they were students.

—·—

Prevent your employees from waiting on line to use the bathroom by getting them to email their supervisor when they need to use the facilities. When the supervisor has a moment, he or she will let the worker know if the facilities are available.

———•———

Have workers to raise their hand when they need to use the bathroom. Knowing that they're being monitored dramatically reduces the amount of time they need to use the facilities.

———•———

Because workers don't have the same standards as bosses, reserve at least one stall and sink for the exclusive use of your executives. This ensures cleanliness and prevents your workers from transmitting any diseases that they're carrying.

———•———

Make your executives more efficient and reduce the time they have to wait to use the bathrooms by getting your employees to line up outside until your managers are finished. This also establishes an office hierarchy and reduces conflicts.

———•———

Let employees know that they're free to use the bathrooms during their breaks and before and after work. Enforce this policy by keeping the facilities locked at all other times.

———•———

Give the bathroom key to a trusted employee and get him or her to store it in a locked cabinet. Have your workers sign for the key when they need to use the facilities.

———•———

Prevent your workers from taking advantage of you by placing a sign-in/signout sheet outside the bathroom. By monitoring how long every employee spends in the bathroom, you can see instantly which employees are wasting time.

———•———

Prevent your clients from stealing staff and corrupting their minds by refusing them access to your facilities.

———•———

Cut the amount of toilet paper, towels and soap you have to buy by training a camera on every dispenser. Fine those who exceed their allocation—or steal your property.

———•———

Reduce your operating costs by deducting a couple of dollars from your workers' paychecks each week to cover the cost of the water and other supplies that they use in the bathroom.

———•———

Install phones in every stall so your employees can continue working while they do their business.

———•———

Improve the overall cleanliness of your bathroom by getting your workers to take turns cleaning them on their own time. Because your employees are the ones who use them, they'll take extra care to ensure that they sparkle.

———•———

Prevent your workers from spending too long in the bathroom by eliminating all janitorial services. Eventually your staff will get the message and do their business before they come to work or after they go home.

———•———

ACTION! ITEMS

- ✗ *ASK!* your workers questions while they do their business.

- ✗ *GIVE!* workers a set number of minutes use the bathroom each day.

- ✗ *RECORD!* each employee's bathroom habits in a spreadsheet.

- ✗ *APPROACH!* workers before they enter the facilities to discuss matters of importance.

- ✗ *ALLOCATE!* every worker a specific time to use the facilities.

- ✗ *ORDER!* workers to email their supervisor when they need to use the bathroom.

- ✗ *HAVE!* workers raise their hand when they want to use the facilities.

- ✗ *RESERVE!* one stall and sink in every bathroom for executives.

- ✗ *GET!* workers to line up outside the bathroom until your executives have finished.

- ✗ *ALLOW!* workers to use the bathrooms only during breaks and before and after work.

- ✗ *STORE!* the bathroom key in a locked closet and get workers to sign for it.

- ✗ *PLACE!* a sign-in/signout sheet outside the facilities.

- ✗ *NEVER!* allow clients to use your workers' bathrooms.

- ✗ *TRAIN!* a camera on dispensers to reduce the amount of toilet paper, soap and towels you have to buy.

- ✗ *REDUCE!* operating costs by deducting the cost of water, electricity and supplies from your workers' paychecks.

- ✗ *INSTALL!* telephones in every stall so your employees can work in the bathroom.

- ✗ *IMPROVE!* office cleanliness by getting your employees to clean the bathrooms.

- ✗ *SAVE!* money and reduce time-wasting by eliminating all janitorial services.

Arranging Office Functions

"A worker is someone who knows nothing about everything."
—Dr. Mark Geoffrey Young

You know how good your workers are at wasting your time. But believe it or not, they're even better when it comes to spending your money—especially when it comes to holding events that honor their coworkers. To make you think they're working, they'll disguise these functions as staff meetings, sales conferences and planning events.

Regardless of what they call the party, you can be sure that it's not only expensive, it's also unnecessary. If you have doubts, move the event to 6:00 p.m. and tell your workers that they're paying for the food and drink, and you'll soon see how important the function really is.

While the do-gooders of the world will lecture you about the importance of team-building events, and talk about how they boost productivity and morale, remember it's your money that's being spent.

By turning the tables and getting your staff to fund their own events, you'll soon find that your workers only need to attend a few "meetings" a year, and the amount of food and drink they need to make these events happen is negligible.

———•———

As much as you may dislike parties, they're an unfortunate part of modern-day office culture. To reduce the amount of time your employees waste, hold all functions after working hours.

———•———

Show your generosity and gain worker acceptance by charging employees less than market price when they want to rent your premises to hold a going-away party or holiday function.

———•———

Support your local college and help train the next generation of leaders by getting their students to cater your office functions.

———•———

Employees often lose their inhibitions at holiday parties. Encourage them to talk about their coworkers by providing them with plenty of alcohol. Use a tape recorder to collect and store this information.

———•———

Recognize your workers by holding an employee appreciation day every year to thank them for everything they've done. Charge a small—but realistic—entry price to gain access to this after-hours function.

———•———

Liquor stores often unload their old wine and scotch on unsuspecting employers. Prevent yourself from being taken advantage of by refusing to serve any alcohol that's more than twelve months old.

———•———

Remember all grapes grow on vines and all wine is made from grapes. Reduce your costs by purchasing the cheapest wine available from your local discounter.

———•———

Ensure a good attendance at your holiday party by telling workers who choose not to attend that they're required to remain at their desks working until quitting time.

———•———

Caterers make their money by over-estimating how much food every worker will eat. Keep your costs under control by reducing the number of people expected by one-third when you place the order.

———•———

Show your staff how valuable they are and recognize their achievements by holding dinners to reward those who help increase your profits. Get your employees to hold a collection to cover the costs.

———•———

Help out your lower-paid workers by selling them any leftovers from your events at cost. Your employees will save money and you'll reduce your overhead.

———•———

If you're holding several functions during the week, keep your costs down by having everything delivered on Monday and storing it until needed. Almost all food lasts longer than the caterer claims.

———•———

Because the food will be unwrapped before the workers arrive, purchase generic snacks, day-old meats and leftovers. Your workers will never know the difference and you'll save money.

———•———

Make life easy on your cleaning staff by holding your holiday party at a worker's house. Compensate this worker by giving him or her an afternoon off on half pay.

———•———

Reduce the costs of your holiday party by holding it just before a critical deadline. Because many workers will be unable to attend, you'll spend less on food, but still get to look good in the eyes of your employees.

———•———

ACTION! ITEMS

- ✗ *HOLD!* all office functions after hours.

- ✗ *RENT!* your premises to employees at a discounted price for office functions.

- ✗ *SUPPORT!* your local college by getting them to cater all of your office functions.

- ✗ *GIVE!* your staff alcohol so they'll talk about their coworkers.

- ✗ *CHARGE!* employees a reasonable fee to attend their Worker Appreciation Day.

- ✗ *REFUSE!* to serve any wine that's more than twelve months old.

- ✗ *PURCHASE!* the most inexpensive wine available at your local liquor store.

- ✗ *FORCE!* workers who don't attend your holiday party to work until quitting time.

- ✗ *REDUCE!* the number of guests expected by one-third when you place a food order.

- ✗ *RECOGNIZE!* staff with after-hours award dinners. Hold a collection to pay for the food.

- ✗ *SELL!* your workers any leftover food at a discount.

- ✗ *HAVE!* your food delivered on Monday and store it until it's needed.

- ✗ *CUT!* costs by serving old food at your employee functions.

- ✗ *HOLD!* your holiday party at a worker's house.

- ✗ *SAVE!* money by holding your holiday party just before a critical deadline.

THE FOOD SITUATION

"Workers today are tyrants. They contradict their bosses, gobble their food, and complain about their clients."
—Dr. Mark Geoffrey Young

Your life would be easy if the only time you had to worry about food was when you held a function. Unfortunately, eating is a big part of your workers' lives, and it can add significant costs to your bottom line and reduce your employees' productivity.

However, with a little bit of planning, you can turn this potential revenue drain into a profit center. Great companies all over the world have turned eating into a huge revenue source by taking control of their employees' food habits.

While preventing your workers from eating during working hours is the logical step, many companies are loathe to do this because they fear huge lawsuits if a worker drops dead from low-blood sugar, or faints from an acute lack of fluids. While these may be legitimate concerns, there are steps you can take to reduce your liability in this area.

———•———

Reduce your costs by eliminating disposable cups and napkins in the kitchen and insisting that workers provide their own coffee cups. If an employee has a visitor, they can bring an extra cup from home or borrow one from a coworker.

———•———

Eliminate the need for your employees to leave the premises during work hours by installing vending machines. Charge the machine owner a fee to cover electricity and rent, as well as a commission on every item sold.

———•———

Ask your workers to run a few errands and pick you up something—anything—for your lunch. Complain loudly about whatever they bring back and refuse to pay for the item.

———•———

Provide only instant coffee to your workers. If your employees complain, remind them that they're free to purchase their own gourmet coffee, decaf, hot chocolate or tea if they don't like the beverages you provide.

———•———

Prevent workers from wasting time by turning the break room into an office and making everybody eat their lunch at their desks. This method is even more efficient if you employ hall monitors to prevent unnecessary conversation during breaks.

———•———

Keep your bug and rodent population down by instituting a policy that prohibits workers from eating at their desks. If you close the break room at the same time, you should be able to eliminate virtually all time wasting.

———•———

Remind your staff that you're the boss by leaving the remains of your lunch in the break room when you've finished eating. Complain frequently about how messy the office is.

———•———

When the weather is nice, workers often use the opportunity to eat lunch outdoors in your parking lot or the company gardens. Eliminate this practice immediately as it can prevent your customers from easily entering and leaving the premises.

———•———

To save money, workers often bring their lunch to work and store their food in your refrigerator, toast their bread in your toaster and use your microwave to heat up their soup. Reduce your electricity costs by eliminating every device that doesn't have a clearly defined business application.

———•———

Help yourself to any of the food in the company refrigerator. If your workers complain, remind them that the only reason the organization has this appliance is due to your generosity.

———•———

Encourage a feeling of belonging by getting your workers to contribute to the cost of beverages by forming a coffee club.

———•———

To generate additional income, stock your vending machines with generic sodas and foods. While this items may be sub-par, they'll sell well because you have a monopoly on what's available on your premises.

———•———

ACTION! ITEMS

✗ *SAVE!* money by eliminating disposable cups and napkins in the kitchen.

✗ *ELIMINATE!* the need for workers to leave the premises by installing vending machines.

✗ *GET!* your workers to run errands and pick up your lunch during their break.

✗ *PROVIDE!* only instant coffee for your workers.

✗ *REDUCE!* time-wasting by forcing your employees to eat lunch at their desk.

✗ *KEEP!* pests under control by preventing workers from eating at their desks.

✗ *HAVE!* your workers run errands during their lunch hour.

✗ *LEAVE!* the remains of your lunch at the table and complain about the mess.

✗ *DON'T!* allow your workers to eat their lunches in the parking lot or your garden area.

✗ *CUT!* electricity costs by eliminating unnecessary devices such as refrigerators and toasters.

✗ *HELP!* yourself to any food your workers have stored in your company's refrigerator.

✗ *FORM!* a club to pay for tea and coffee.

✗ *STOCK!* your vending machines with generic products to maximize revenues.

Running Effective Meetings

*"The important thing in a worker is how quickly they achieve
the goals you set for them, not what they learn along the way."*
—*Dr. Mark Geoffrey Young*

While almost all meetings are a complete waste of time, they
don't have to be. Every meeting can be productive if you
implement a few simple rules of conduct and discipline, and
ensure that they're followed to the letter.

The main reason that meetings are useless is because your
workers already know what's going to be discussed. Prevent
this from happening by instituting a code of silence that
prohibits your workers from speaking to each other after 8:00
a.m. or before 5:00 p.m.

But be warned. This policy does have a downside. Because most employees feel that they're entitled to discuss business with their coworkers, they'll stretch out each meeting for as long as possible, reducing the effectiveness of your talk-free workplace. Eliminate this temptation by fining workers who speak for more than a minute, talk out of turn or discuss matters that you deem to be of no interest to anybody.

———•———

Reduce disruptions during the workday by scheduling all meetings for 5:00 p.m. Friday, so your employees can use the weekend to get a head start on next week's work.

———•———

Every boss knows that meetings are a waste of time. Make yourself more efficient by turning up for every meeting fifteen minutes late and popping in and out.

———•———

Make your meetings more effective by insisting that everyone turn up on time by starting the meeting exactly when it's scheduled. Allow latecomers to listen to the proceedings on the intercom.

———•———

Ensure all your workers are on an equal footing at your meetings by arranging seating alphabetically—regardless of the shape of the room or who needs to speak.

———•———

Prevent yourself from being rushed into a bad decision by deferring anything that could cause controversy, damage the company or impact your sales until the next meeting.

———•———

Make sure your workers get the most out of every meeting by asking participants random questions and having an employee summarize all of the important points before anybody leaves the room.

———•———

Never allow your employees to eat or drink during meetings as it prevents them getting a full grasp of what's going on. This can also lead to misunderstandings later as most workers cannot think and chew at the same time.

———•———

Ensure that the person leading the meeting is given the respect he or she deserves by demanding that all workers address them as Mr. or Ms. Chairperson.

———•———

Insist that workers who are unable to attend the meeting call in by telephone to participate—regardless of their responsibilities, where they're located, or the time at their location.

———•———

Emphasize the importance of the weekly meeting by insisting that it take place at the same time and place each week—even if there's nothing to discuss.

———•———

Meetings are the perfect opportunity to catch up on work and email. Use your Blackberry and laptop to the fullest—your employees will fill you in if you miss something.

———•———

Make your staff feel good by asking for their opinions just before you leave the meeting. Because you're on your way out, have them put their thoughts in writing and email them to you so you can give them the consideration they deserve.

———•———

Hold brainstorming meetings frequently and let your workers know how you feel about these events by looking supremely bored when people put forward their ideas. Feel free to complain about their lack of creativity.

———•———

Use your company meetings to improve morale. Instead of using the time to look at the big picture, concentrate on the small, insignificant issues that really upset your workers.

———•———

Whenever an employee comes up with an idea at a meeting, go into great detail about why it won't work and why it's not worthy of consideration. Get your other workers to reinforce your opinions with their criticisms.

———•———

If a worker claims that one of your ideas won't work, get them to put all their objections in writing to prevent the meeting from getting bogged down in details.

———•———

Only let senior management speak at company meetings—and only on topics that you find relevant. Allowing every employee to participate is a sure-fire recipe for chaos.

———•———

Support your workers who make a big sale, acquire a new client, or achieve a milestone by allowing them to speak for one minute at your meeting. Get them to emphasize how your support made their success possible.

———•———

Avoid problem-solving meetings, as these events always become a venue for employees to vent their frustrations and complain about management. The easy way to eliminate problems is to eliminate meetings.

———•———

Keep your meetings short by only allowing workers to speak for a total of three minutes during each meeting—regardless of the topic, their expertise, or how many employees are present.

———•———

To ensure that you get your point of view across, speak for as long as necessary. After you've finished, go around the room and get each worker to explain what you said and what they're required to do.

———•———

ACTION! ITEMS

- ✔ *SCHEDULE!* all meetings for 5:00 p.m. Friday.
- ✔ *TURN!* up late to meetings and pop in and out.
- ✔ *ALLOW!* latecomers to listen to the meeting on the intercom.
- ✔ *ARRANGE!* seating alphabetically at meetings.
- ✔ *DELAY!* all controversial decisions.
- ✔ *HAVE!* an employee summarize the meeting.
- ✔ *NEVER!* allow participants to eat or drink at meetings.
- ✔ *INSIST!* that your workers address the meeting leader as Mr. or Ms. Chairperson.
- ✔ *GET!* absent workers to phone in to the meeting.
- ✔ *HOLD!* the weekly meeting at the same time each week—even if there's nothing to discuss.
- ✔ *USE!* meetings to catch up on your email and other tasks.
- ✔ *INSIST!* that all workers submit all their ideas in writing.
- ✔ *LOOK!* bored at all brainstorming meetings and complain about the lack of creativity.
- ✔ *SPEND!* a lot of time looking at small, insignificant issues.
- ✔ *INSIST!* that all ideas submitted by staff will not work.
- ✔ *IF!* a worker objects to your idea, get them to put their comments in writing.
- ✔ *ALLOW!* only senior staff to speak at meetings.
- ✔ *LET!* workers who make a big sale speak for one minute.
- ✔ *AVOID!* problem-solving meetings.
- ✔ *ONLY!* allow workers to speak for a total of three minutes.
- ✔ *SPEAK!* for as long as necessary to get your point across.

Traveling On Business

"Show me a worker with a goal and I'll laugh. Show me a boss without a goal and I'll show you a middle manager."—Dr. Mark Geoffrey Young

Meetings are one way to waste time. Business travel is another. Your workers know that when they're out of the office your ability to check up on them is limited. As a result, they'll use the opportunity to goof off, visit relatives, catch up on their shopping (which they'll bill you for) and visit restaurants that are well beyond their means.

To put it gently, your workers see business travel as a mini-vacation—but better—because you're paying for it. That's right, not only do your employees get away from the office, they get a break from their crying children, nagging spouses and annoying coworkers.

And, it gets even better for your worker. Not only do you have to pay their salary while they're traveling, you're also forced to pick up their accommodation, transportation and incidental costs. As a result, your workers use this opportunity to line their pockets with your gold and spend, spend, spend.

———•———

Give your workers extra assignments to complete while they're flying. Remind them that just because you're paying for their airfare, doesn't mean they're allowed to watch movies and dine on the gourmet fare the airline provides.

———•———

Inform your traveling workers that you still expect them to complete their normal work while they're visiting clients. After all, almost every hotel room comes with a desk.

———•———

Have your clients sign a statement showing how long they spent with your worker. Many employees pad their trips with additional meetings so they can stay away longer than needed.

———•———

Never pay for your employees' phone calls while they're traveling. Just about everything can wait until they return home.

———•———

Let workers know that they're still expected to work their normal business hours—and remain contactable—regardless of what time it is where they're staying.

———•———

Encourage your workers to save money by eliminating all travel advances. Paying expenses thirty days after they're submitted allows your employees to deposit the check into their bank account and watch their savings grow.

———•———

Insist that your workers submit all reimbursement requests within seven days of incurring an expense. Refusing to accept claims outside this period will dramatically improve your cash flow.

———•———

Prevent workers from goofing off when they're traveling by issuing them time sheets to detail their activities. This will let you see exactly how much time they spend working.

———•———

Charge workers who visit friends or relatives a portion of the trip's cost. After all, it's only fair that they pay their share if they turn a business trip into a vacation.

———•———

Give your workers unlimited travel cards for the buses and trains so they can explore the city when they're traveling. Not only will you save money on expensive cabs, they'll get to see first-hand how the locals live.

———•———

Stop your workers from going into debt when they travel by having them charge everything to their personal credit card. After they receive the bill, get them to submit it to your accounts payable department.

———•———

Get your workers to share your cash flow problems by paying expenses on the 30th of the month after they're submitted.

———•———

Stop workers from stealing your money by requiring receipts for every expense they incur. If they claim that the local bus service didn't issue a receipt, allow them to submit a notarized statement to this effect.

———•———

Workers specialize in taking advantage of your generosity by inflating payments such as tips. Eliminate this scam by insisting that your employees to pay for these optional gratuities themselves.

—•—

Get workers to pay for their own meals when they're traveling. Remind them that since they have to eat at home, their meals are not your responsibility.

—•—

Prevent your workers who are traveling together from getting lonely by getting them to share a room with a coworker. Some hotels even offer cots, so you can double or triple their fun and allow them to party all night.

—•—

Book your workers who are traveling alone into a youth hostel to prevent from feeling isolated. This not only takes their mind off their loneliness, it also helps them make new friends.

—•—

Make travel fun for your workers by getting them to stay just outside the city limits. They'll feel good about saving you a few dollars, and get to see an area of the city that few tourists visit.

—•—

Reduce your travel costs by booking your workers into independent hotels and motels. Well-known chains charge a lot more than their unbranded siblings to cover their advertising costs.

—•—

ACTION! ITEMS

✗ *GIVE!* your workers extra assignments to complete during their flight.

✗ *TELL!* workers that they're still expected to complete their regular work while traveling.

✗ *GET!* your clients to sign statements certifying that they actually met with your worker.

✗ *DO!* not pay for traveling workers' personal phone calls.

✗ *HAVE!* employees work their regular hours, regardless of the time at their new location.

✗ *ELIMINATE!* all travel advances.

✗ *REFUSE!* to pay expenses that are more than seven days old.

✗ *ISSUE!* workers time sheets so they can detail their activities while traveling.

✗ *CHARGE!* workers who visit friends or relatives a portion of the trip's cost.

✗ *GIVE!* employees vouchers for public transport so they can see the city they're visiting.

✗ *INSIST!* that your workers charge all expenses to their personal credit cards.

✗ *PAY!* expenses on the 30th of the month after they're submitted.

✗ *DEMAND!* receipts or notarized statements for all expenses.

✗ *FORCE!* workers to pay tips themselves as these are optional.

✗ *NEVER!* reimburse workers for meals when they're traveling.

✗ *ALLOW!* those employees who are traveling together to share a hotel room.

✗ *PREVENT!* loneliness by booking workers into a youth hostel so they can make new friends.

✗ *PLACE!* workers in hotels just outside the city limits so they can discover attractions that are off the beaten track.

✗ *LET!* your employees stay at independent, unbranded hotels.

YOUR COMPANY AND THE COMMUNITY

"Life is one big obstacle course and your workers will be your biggest obstacle if you don't run them down whenever you can."
—Dr. Mark Geoffrey Young

Even though you're in business to make money, you'll probably need to get involved with at least one community organization if you want to maximize your profits. While this may appear to be a waste of time, it's essential if you want to appeal to a wide cross-section of the population.

Despite the fact that you need to put every cent your company earns into your pocket, you'll generate more business if you make at least a token effort to give something back. Even though your time is too valuable to waste volunteering, there's nothing stopping you claiming credit for the good work your employees do. While this may appear unfair, face facts. You're entitled to the credit. The only reason your workers can get involved with their communities is because you allow them to take some nights and weekends off.

As well as getting involved with local organizations, it's important to get your workers to know your family. Allowing them to bond with your children and visit your home lets them see how the other half lives. While they may be jealous because they know that they'll never achieve your status, it gives them something to dream about.

———•———

Regardless of how small your town is, there are a number of organizations looking for help. Make it easy for your workers to donate by pre-screening these non-profits and circulating donation sheets for those charities you support.

———•———

Get your workers involved with your family by allowing them to baby-sit your children on nights and weekends. Tell them you won't be offended if they bring along some work to complete after your kids fall asleep.

———•———

If one of your children fails to achieve his or her potential, get a worker with expertise in that area to tutor them. Base this worker's bonus on how well your child does.

———•———

Have your workers teach your children how to do their jobs. Tell them that while their positions are secure, you do intend to pass the business on to your children. As a result, it's essential that your kids know what everybody does—even if they haven't yet graduated from elementary school.

———•———

Never get involved in your workers' personal lives. Remind them that while you would love to support their fundraisers, and help the organizations their children belong to, you're unable to get involved due to the possibility of harassment charges being levied against you.

———·———

Allow your children to approach workers directly for causes they're involved with. Point out to your employees how your children will feel if they don't win the prize for raising the most money, selling the most cookies or getting the most sponsors for their walkathon.

———·———

Get your workers' families involved with your company by holding frequent "Bring Your Children To Work Days." Let the children know that you expect them to show their gratitude by performing worthwhile tasks such as stuffing envelopes, preparing presentations and running errands.

———·———

Make your company more profitable by allowing charities to place donation cans in your lunchrooms and in the public areas of your business. Use these donations to reduce your taxable income.

———·———

Give small donations to as many community organizations as possible so you can use their logos on your stationery and signage. If you choose the right organizations, their members will patronize your company and the increased business will more than pay for your tax-deductible donations.

———·———

Support your local high schools and colleges by letting their students work as interns during your busy periods. As well as reducing your labor costs, you'll help the students get real-world training that will make it easier for them to get a job when they graduate.

———•———

Increase the size of your donations by allowing charities to use your premises for their meetings rent-free. This allows you to claim the rent you didn't receive as a tax deduction.

———•———

Help your workers keep their family together by randomly testing everyone for drugs on a monthly basis. Not only will you stop them overdosing, you'll prevent them from wasting their money on illegal substances.

———•———

Encourage your workers to take part in community activities on their own time and allow them to display the awards they win in your reception area. Remember, it's your willingness to give them weekends and nights off that makes it possible for them to get these awards.

———•———

When a worker is given an award for volunteering, issue a press release so the whole town can see how you encourage your workers to play an active role in their local community.

———•———

ACTION! ITEMS

- ✗ *CIRCULATE!* donation sheets so your workers can support the causes you believe in.

- ✗ *ALLOW!* your workers to baby-sit your children at night and on weekends.

- ✗ *BASE!* your workers' bonuses on how well your children do at school.

- ✗ *GET!* your workers to teach their jobs to your children.

- ✗ *NEVER!* get involved in your workers' causes or charities.

- ✗ *PERMIT!* your children to approach your workers directly to support their causes.

- ✗ *ENCOURAGE!* workers to bring their family to work when you're short-handed.

- ✗ *PUT!* donation cans throughout your offices to reduce your taxable income.

- ✗ *GENERATE!* extra business by placing the logos of community groups on your signs and stationery.

- ✗ *USE!* students as interns whenever possible.

- ✗ *LET!* charities use your premises so you can claim a tax deduction on the rent they didn't pay.

- ✗ *ENCOURAGE!* families to bond by testing your workers each month for illegal drugs.

- ✗ *DISPLAY!* all of the community awards your staff win in the reception area.

- ✗ *SHOW!* your support by issuing a press release whenever a worker wins an award.

BUILDING YOUR COMPANY'S CULTURE

"When a worker believes he or she can, and the boss believes that he or she can't, the boss is always right."—Dr. Mark Geoffrey Young

When it comes to dealing with your workers, you must realize that not only are they not very bright, they're incapable of making rational decisions. While this observation may appear harsh, remember, if they were as smart as you, they'd be the boss and you'd be the worker.

As a result, you need to set the standards and create your organization's culture. When building a company culture, it's important to remember that workers need constant instruction. This means you must tell them everything: where the bathrooms are, which stalls they can use, when they can go to lunch, which brand of pen to use and whether the shades should be up or down. While this may appear to be overkill, don't forget—the minute you let workers make decisions is the beginning of your downfall.

To ensure that everyone is on the same page, many companies produce expensive employee manuals and guides that they fill with detailed rules and instructions. This is totally unnecessary and a complete waste of money. Remember, your company is young, it's constantly evolving, and the rules that apply today may not apply tomorrow.

———•———

Snap your fingers when you need to summon a worker. Committing your employees' names to memory is a waste of time—most workers will leave at the first possible opportunity.

———•———

Whenever you encounter employees holding a conversation, remind them that all discussions are to take place in officially sanctioned meetings.

———•———

If you have an urgent task, spend a lot of time explaining why it's important, exactly how it should be completed, and why it must be on your desk at 9:00 a.m. tomorrow.

———•———

Never waste time checking business cards before they're printed. Printers have great spelling and the worker can always pay to have their cards reprinted if they're unhappy with the result.

———•———

When an employee is working on a task in an area where you have absolutely no knowledge, sit with them to offer input and encouragement.

———•———

Make your carpets last longer by insisting that your workers and customers take off their shoes before entering your premises. As well as reducing your future refurbishment costs, you'll also spend less on cleaning.

———•———

Listen to all of your workers' phone calls, monitor their emails and eavesdrop on their conversations. Not only will this expand your knowledge about your employees, it will come in useful if you ever get sued or have to fire an employee.

———•———

Protect your workers from evil by opening all mail and packages—including those marked personal—as they enter your premises. Remind your employees that anything delivered to your address belongs to the company.

———•———

While your workers are required to conduct all their personal business after work, you may sometimes need to handle personal matters during company hours. Feel free to cut your toenails, iron your clothes or brush your teeth when issuing instructions to your employees.

———•———

Keep your company's reputation intact by insisting that every piece of work cross your desk before it's sent to a client. Call workers frequently to question their methodology and prevent mistakes.

———•———

Use desktop publishing to the fullest, and show your workers how flexible the technology is by continuing to edit documents after they've been laid out and approved by the client.

———•———

Take full credit for everything your employees accomplish. After all, it's your existence that makes their jobs possible.

———•———

Prevent office leaks by using the telephone and email as little as possible. Instead, set up a face-to-face meeting to discuss every matter—no matter how trivial it may appear.

———•———

Stay in touch with changing market conditions by instituting frequent employee reorganizations. As well as keeping you in touch with what's happening, it prevents your workers from becoming complacent.

———•———

Keep yourself in the loop by practicing management by walking around. Not only will you catch mistakes before they occur, you'll be able to make your workers more efficient by constantly looking over their shoulders.

———•———

Prevent your workers from getting distracted by instating a clean desk policy. Personal photographs and memorabilia cloud your employees thinking and prevent them from doing their jobs.

———•———

Reduce theft by searching your workers' bags each night before they leave the premises. Confiscate anything that could belong to the company if the worker doesn't have a receipt to prove they purchased it.

———•———

Make life easy for your kitchen and outdoor workers by giving them one hundred percent polyester uniforms that don't need ironing.

———•———

Prevent the competition from infiltrating your offices by requiring all of your workers to carry their official company identification at all times. Do not allow employees to enter the premises without their ID—even if you know them personally.

———•———

When an employee loses a loved one, show your human side by casually mentioning how sorry you are to hear about their loss as you pass them in the hallway. Ask them how this death will affect their work.

———•———

ACTION! ITEMS

- ✗ *SNAP!* your fingers whenever you need to summon a worker.

- ✗ *ALLOW!* conversations to take place only in official meetings.

- ✗ *EXPLAIN!* even the simplest tasks in great detail.

- ✗ *NEVER!* check business cards before they're printed.

- ✗ *OFFER!* advice even if you have no knowledge of the subject.

- ✗ *HAVE!* everybody remove their shoes before they enter your premises.

- ✗ *MONITOR!* phone calls, emails and personal conversations.

- ✗ *OPEN!* all packages and letters when they enter the premises.

- ✗ *CUT!* your nails and brush your teeth when speaking to your workers.

- ✗ *EXAMINE!* every piece of work produced by your employees.

- ✗ *EDIT!* documents after they've been laid out and approved.

- ✗ *TAKE!* credit for everything good your company does.

- ✗ *PREVENT!* leaks by using the telephone as little as possible.

- ✗ *HAVE!* frequent reorganizations to keep workers on their toes.

- ✗ *WALK!* around the office and make frequent suggestions.

- ✗ *FORCE!* workers to remove all memorabilia from their desks.

- ✗ *SEARCH!* your workers bags before they leave the premises.

- ✗ *GIVE!* kitchen workers polyester uniforms.

- ✗ *INSIST!* that all workers carry their company ID at all times.

- ✗ *WHEN!* a worker loses a loved one, mention how sad you are as you pass them in the hallway.

DEALING WITH MISTAKES

"A worker who makes a mistake does not earn a living for very long."
—Dr. Mark Geoffrey Young

Every worker thinks mistakes are a part of life. Why? Employees are responsible for 97.2 percent of all blunders made in the workplace. If this number sounds unbelievable, face facts: when was the last time you made a mistake?

If you think it's not possible to decrease the number of errors your workers make, think again. Many progressive, innovative and cutting edge companies are reducing their costs by forcing their workers to pay for everything they botch up. While this works, it's not the best solution. To totally eliminate mistakes, get every employee to pay for their coworkers errors—even if they're not involved.

While this may appear harsh, it's effective. Because every employee is forced to pay for their workmates' sloppiness, they'll keep an eye on each other. Since mistakes now affect everybody—the number of errors made by your workers will fall to virtually zero. And, if you're worried that this policy won't be won't be popular, relax, you're not running for office.

———•———

When an employee makes a mistake, no matter how minor, chastise him or her in front of everybody. Not only will you prevent the worker from making the same error twice, all of their coworkers will see how this employee let the team down.

———•———

Even though you can never be proven wrong, if a worker discovers an error in something that you did, make the change and shrug off the comment. Tell the worker that it's only a small detail that doesn't change your opinion.

———•———

Reduce the possibility of mistakes by sitting next to an employee as he or she works and issue instructions as they tackle each task. The worker will appreciate your input.

———•———

Improve your company's profitability by implementing changes that failed at your competition. You have better management and your workers won't make the same mistakes.

———•———

Blame every error on somebody else because you're the boss. Remember, you don't make mistakes. If an employee claims otherwise, fire him or her. This reduces the likelihood of other workers challenging you and allows you to live a peaceful existence.

———•———

Remember that even your most experienced workers do not have your skills or intelligence. To encourage them to learn, look over their shoulders as you pass their desk and offer creative input to help them get it right.

———•———

When you can't find anything wrong with an employee's work, just state that you're not happy with it. This keeps him or her on their toes and forces them to worker harder.

———•———

Ensure that your workers learn from their mistakes by pointing them out in front of clients. Then apologize to the customer for not having employees who are up to the task.

———•———

Show staff you're keeping an eye on everything by using your company meetings to bring up mistakes, criticize workers and determine punishments.

———•———

Most workers feel undervalued. Prevent this from happening by running everything by them. This not only improves their morale, it allows you to blame things on more people.

———•———

When editing a document, make your corrections in purple, green or yellow pen so they stand out. Prevent your workers from getting hurt by writing your comments very small, so they don't think that you're yelling at them.

———•———

Every time an employee makes a mistake, replace them with a temp to show your other employees how easy everybody is to replace.

———•———

ACTION! ITEMS

 ✗ *CHASTISE!* workers in public when they make a mistake.

 ✗ *IF!* you make an error, make the change but tell the worker that it doesn't affect your opinion.

 ✗ *SIT!* with employees as they work to reduce mistakes.

 ✗ *IMPLEMENT!* changes that failed at other companies as you have better management skills.

 ✗ *BLAME!* every error you make on somebody else.

 ✗ *LOOK!* over your workers' shoulders and make suggestions as you pass their desks.

 ✗ *INFORM!* your workers you're unhappy with their work, but don't give any specifics.

 ✗ *POINT!* out your workers' mistakes in front of clients.

 ✗ *BRING!* up worker mistakes and dish out punishments at your staff meetings.

 ✗ *RUN!* as much as possible by each worker so you'll have more people to blame.

 ✗ *USE!* very small handwriting and brightly colored pens to edit documents.

 ✗ *REPLACE!* those employees who make mistakes with temporary workers.

SAYING GOODBYE TO YOUR WORKERS

*"Nothing can be achieved without great bosses: no matter
how hard they try, workers can never achieve greatness."*
—Dr. Mark Geoffrey Young

Even though you offer your workers near-utopian working
conditions, many of your good employees will depart for greener
pastures, while the deadbeats will hang around until you force
them to move on. Regardless of how the employee leaves, tell
your remaining workers that it was your decision.

While departing workers can cause short-term pain,
remember, not only are your employees your least valuable
resource, they're easy to replace. Instead of expressing concern
when a worker quits, tell your remaining employees that you're
relieved. Point out how overpaid the "fired" employee was.

Let them know how much easier their jobs will be because they'll be carrying less dead wood. And finally, remind your remaining workers that if they don't shape up, they too will be shown the door.

After you escort the departing worker from the premises, take your time finding a replacement. The longer you take to fill the position, the greater your profits. And, when you eventually fill the vacancy, remember your former employee was overpaid and under-worked, so their replacement will work harder and cost you less.

———•———

When a worker is fired, forget to mention that you let the employee go to the remaining staff. Telling your workers that an employee is no longer part of the team will only encourage them to worry about their positions.

———•———

Keep your employees on their toes by running ads for every position in your company at least twice a year. This makes it easy to replace inefficient workers—and encourages everybody to work harder.

———•———

Make all exit interviews personal. Use this final opportunity to point out all of the departing worker's faults and let him or her know that you've been carrying them for years.

———•———

Reduce your costs by eliminating a worker's cell phone and email account before you actually fire him or her.

———•———

Remove a worker's nameplate from their cubicle before you let him or her go. Having a former employee's name on the wall will remind your remaining workers that this person once worked for you.

———•———

When you fire a worker, do it after your other employees have gone home. When they see a new person in the former worker's seat the next day, they'll assume he or she is on vacation.

———•———

Prevent your workers worrying about their futures by refusing to comment on rumors—even if they're false. Your employees aren't going to believe anything that comes out of your mouth.

———•———

Reduce your stress levels by delegating unpleasant tasks such as firing workers to your management trainees. They'll not only get assertiveness training, they'll also see how difficult your job is.

———•———

Regardless of how long a worker has been with you, their contribution to the company, or why you're letting them go, never offer the departing employee a severance package. Doing so gives the worker an inflated view of their true value.

———•———

When you let a worker go, simply say "you're fired" and call security. Allowing a fired worker to return to their desk will cause a scene and disrupt your office's productivity.

———•———

Reduce your unemployment costs by challenging a worker's benefits—even when you're wrong. If your ex-employees see that you're playing hardball, they'll simply get another job.

———•———

ACTION! ITEMS

- ✗ NEVER! let employees know that you fired a worker.

- ✗ RUN! ads frequently for every position in your company.

- ✗ POINT! out all of a worker's faults at their exit interview.

- ✗ CUT! costs by canceling email and cell phone accounts before you fire a worker.

- ✗ REMOVE! a worker's name from their cubicle or office before you fire them.

- ✗ FIRE! a worker at the end of the day so your remaining workers will think he or she is on vacation.

- ✗ NEVER! comment on rumors as your staff will not believe anything you say.

- ✗ DELEGATE! unpleasant tasks such as firing a worker to a management trainee.

- ✗ NEVER! offer a worker a severance package.

- ✗ PREVENT! disruptions to your office routine by refusing to allow fired workers to return to their desks.

- ✗ ALWAYS! challenge an employee's right to unemployment—even if you're wrong.

ACKNOWLEDGEMENTS

"God gives us our relatives—thank God we can choose our employees."
—Dr. Mark Geoffrey Young

Writing a book is always a team effort due of the large number of people involved. Until I started this project I had no idea how many people were willing to help me out for free—including those who had absolutely no idea who I was (a very, very big thank you to Dick DeBartolo for writing the foreword).

And while I promised to thank everybody, there's no way to avoid missing somebody. So, if you made a contribution to this book, let me know how demotivated you are and I'll include you in the next version.

Because many of the people who helped me out work for organizations that would scream if they knew that their corporate secrets were out in the world, I'm not going to say what anybody actually did, needless to say some people gave me tips, others provided insight and inspiration, while others fed me when I was hungry.

Here's the list (in alphabetical order): Zach Auslander, Sharon Behnke, Carole Bleicher, Helen Boltson, Hazel Bradley, Zippy Collins, Ben Curry, Andy Clarke, Stephen Colbert, Mark Day, Dick DeBartolo, Nick Denton, Fred Dieckamp, William Hammond, Tracee Hines, Ralph Gammon, Ellen Greenberg, Ruth Mostern, John Oakley, Randy Patrick, Shirley Pon-Dieckamp, Greg Rapport, Barbara Schancupp, Marvin

Schancupp, Pam Schancupp, Carl Schell, David Seto, Jules Smirke, Harvey Spencer, Leslie Spencer, Jon Stewart, Susan Weintraub, Elaine Weiss, Laura Wenzell, Diane Young, Kristen Young, Mike Young, Robert Young.

If you bought a copy of the book, thank you. If you bought the personalized version of this book, a double thank you. And if you bought the personalized hard cover, a triple thank you. And if you're a book reviewer who gave this book a positive review—what can I say but your contribution is the best gift I could ever hope to receive.

Before I go, a special thank you to Jackson, the cutest baby ever, who arrived eight weeks early and threw everything into chaos—but all is forgiven.

ABOUT THE AUTHOR

Dr. Mark G. Young is an accomplished journalist, author, public speaker, entrepreneur, educator, leader and creative thinker of the most extraordinary kind. His career began while still in high school when he began selling belt buckles by mail order through Australia's leading CB radio magazine.

After graduating high school, Young took the first steps to establishing a retail empire when he launched Perth's first—and only—newspaper headline printing operation in two of the city's biggest weekend markets.

Bitten by the media bug, Young abandoned all thoughts of a career in retail, and launched Australian Alternatives, a small, but influential, newsmagazine with a readership of almost two-thousand in all Australian states.

After its five-issue run, Young left his native Perth for Sydney where he set up The School of Journalism, an independent college that trained almost three-hundred students over a five-year period.

While attempting to build the School of Journalism into a cutting edge educational institution, he simultaneously created the impressive-sounding World Press Service, a news organization that provided freelance articles to some fifty publications in Australia, New Zealand, England and the United States.

After obtaining his Doctorate of Divinity from the now-defunct Church of Gospel Ministry, in Chula Vista, CA, the newly titled Dr. Young headed to New York. In the Big Apple, Dr.

Young revived the World Press Service by providing a weekly commentary about life in the USA to Australia's ABC radio network. While living the life of a radio personality, Young launched Celebrity Tours, which showed both locals and tourists the New York City addresses of some of the country's biggest TV and movie stars. He perfected his management techniques and put them into practice in the Häagen-Dazs franchise he owned on Manhattan's exclusive Upper East Side.

When not educating business leaders about the benefits of demotivation, Dr. Young lives quietly in New York with his wife and son, who prefer to remain anonymous. His other books include How to Promote Your Business and The West Australian Joke Book. As well as his doctorate, Young possesses a Bachelor of Arts (Communication) from Western Australia's Murdoch University.

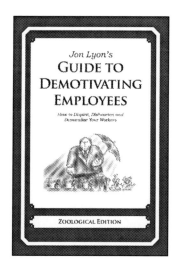

If you'd like to get even more value from Dr. Young's Guide to Demotivating Employees, why not order a personalized copy to send to your friends, relatives and employees. Not only will they learn the benefits of demotivation, they'll think you're brilliant because it will have your name on it. That's right. Even though you may barely be able to sign your name, you can have your name on the title for just a bit more than the standard edition.

But the value doesn't end there. Not only will you have your name printed on the cover, you'll also be able to dedicate it to a person of your choosing and include twenty-five of the people who demotivate you the most. How much would you expect to pay for this? Don't answer yet, because there's more.

As well as getting your name on the cover, a dedication to the person of your choice and a list of the twenty-five people who demotivate you the most, you'll also get a bonus chapter of tips to wring even more out of your employees than you ever thought possible. And for those of you who know true value, you can even order this book in hardcover.

Prices start at only $25.95 (even less for large orders) for the soft-cover edition and $45.95 (also less for large orders) for the hard-cover version. What are you waiting for? Go to www.dolyttle.com to order your copy now.

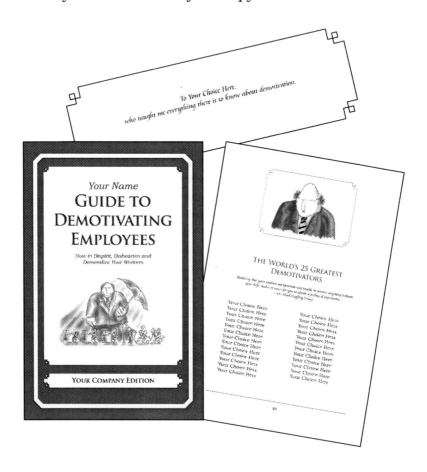

ORDER! FORM

Dolyttle & Seamore
345 West 85th Street Suite 43
New York, NY 10024
917-734-7892 • info@dolyttle.com
(For faster service go to www.dolyttle.com)

Name

Address   Apt.

City   State   ZIP

Country

Email

Phone

Prices

Softcover (Standard Edition)	
$12.95 plus $4.00 per book shipping and handling	
Softcover (Personalized Edition)	
1 to 10 books	$29.95 plus $4.00 per book shipping
11 to 25 books	$27.95 plus $2.00 per book shipping
26 + books	$25.95 plus shipping (varies by location)
Hardcover (Personalized Edition)	
1 to 10 books	$59.95 plus $4.00 per book shipping
11 to 25 books	$49.95 plus $2.00 per book shipping
26+ books	$45.95 plus shipping (varies by location)

Please send me:

_____ books at $_____ each plus $_____

shipping. *(NY residents add 8.375% sales tax)* Total $_____.

Continues over

Title: _____'s
    Guide to Demotivating Employees

Edition: _____ Edition

Dedicated To _____.

The World's 25 Greatest Demotivators

_____	_____
_____	_____
_____	_____
_____	_____
_____	_____
_____	_____
_____	_____
_____	_____
_____	_____
_____	_____
_____	_____
_____	_____
_____	

If you don't have twenty-five people who demotivate you, don't worry. Simply write your top demotivators in the blanks, and we'll fill in the remaining spaces.

www.dolyttle.com

Lightning Source UK Ltd.
Milton Keynes UK
UKOW031128261112

202779UK00002B/294/A